TESTIMONY

The writing of this book was sparked by the testimony of how God's plan for spiritual order and authority in the family was received and applied by some very special new friends of mine. Their story is as follows:

> "For years, my husband and I searched for resources to help with parenting our three children in a godly and biblical way. Some were helpful but nothing was completely or exactly what we needed until the Lord led us to Barb and the material she presents in this new book, *Spiritual Protection and Deliverance for our Children*.
>
> My husband and I were both raised in Christian homes, but we still struggled to understand how to guide our children spiritually and support their emotional needs. Our boys wrestled with emotional issues very early on and our home quickly became one of constant dysregulation and disorder. Both our boys have ADHD, and our younger boy was diagnosed with sensory processing disorder. He exhibited out-of-control rage, anger, and physical and verbal aggression. At times, he became unsafe toward himself and others at home. We saw psychologists and neurologists who advised us to put him on medication and were told that he was hard wired to be defiant, and that this would be his normal. However, I knew as his mother that

underneath it all, he was a kind, compassionate and sensitive boy who was just misunderstood.

I dove deep into research and therapies to help understand the heart behind my sweet boy's behavior. It consumed our whole family life as we tried to find ways to support our children. Our son struggled with sleep and night terrors. He complained of stomach pain constantly and would throw up frequently. Eventually all his relationships were affected by his aggressive behaviors including close family. It greatly affected family activities, holidays, and church attendance. He refused to go to school, and his behavior was so unpredictable that we did not feel safe leaving our home with him. Our sweet boy spent most of his days screaming and violently out of control, then falling into a cycle of shame and remorse. His sense of identity was shattered, and he began to take on the labels placed on him. Anxiety and depression started to grow deeper and more severe in him and in myself. I felt so alone and isolated in my circumstances.

Finally, we had exhausted all resources and still were not better off than before until we connected with Barb. Barb came to our home and taught us the connection between mind, body, and spirit. We learned that all our struggles linked back to the main issue which was spiritual bondage.

Through Barb's willingness to meet with us and the biblical teachings and prayers in her most recent book, *Position Yourself for Healing*, the spiritual realm became unveiled to us. We learned how to step into spiritual authority and protection for our children.

My husband and I began to stand together against the enemy in prayer and find freedom for ourselves and our children. Through prayer, our son also received freedom from the dysregulation, sensory problems and hypersensitivity that had caused him to have physical aggression, violent outbursts and rage. He can now regulate and enjoy family activities and outings. He has made friends and is thriving at school. He shows so much compassion to those around him and even in his hard moments no longer shows aggression toward others. God has allowed his brilliance to emerge, and it is a delight to watch our kids grow into the people God created them to be.

We are now operating in a new level of spiritual parenting I never thought was even possible. Our home is calmer, more regulated, and less stressful. No longer do we fearfully spend hours waiting and trying to get rage to subside; instead, we pick up our swords and engage in the battle. God has done miraculous things in our family, and we have never enjoyed parenting more than we do now."

~Rebecca Hope

"The righteous cry out, and the LORD hears, And delivers them out of all their troubles. The LORD is near to those who have a broken heart, And saves such as have a contrite spirit."
Psalm 34: 17-18

Many blessings,
Barbara Jane

Spiritual
PROTECTION
and
DELIVERANCE
for our
CHILDREN

©2025 Barbara De Simon

Published in Windsor, Ontario, Canada by Barbara De Simon

All rights reserved. This book is protected by the copyright laws of Canada. No part of this publication may be reproduced, stored in a retrieval system, or transmitted in any form or by any means—electronic, mechanical, photocopy, recording or any other–except for brief quotations, without prior permission of the author/publisher.

This book is not intended to be a substitute for the advice of medical professionals such as physicians, psychiatrists, psychologists, counsellors, therapists, or any other professional. It is the responsibility of the reader to seek professional help when needed, at their discretion.

Scripture quotations identified as NIV® are from the New International Version®. Copyright © 1973, 1978, 1984, 2011 by Biblica, Inc.™ Used by permission. All rights reserved worldwide.

Scripture quotations identified as NKJV are from the New King James Version®. Copyright © 1982 by Thomas Nelson, Inc. Used by permission. All rights reserved.

Scripture quotations marked NLT are taken from the Holy Bible, New Living Translation, copyright 1996, 2004.

Scripture quotations marked NASB are from the New American Standard Bible. Copyright © 1960, 1962, 1963, 1968, 1971, 1972, 1973, 1975, 1977 by The Lockman Foundation. Used by permission.

Scripture quotations marked ESV are from The ESV® Bible (The Holy Bible, English Standard Version®), © 2001 by Crossway, a publishing ministry of Good News Publishers. Used by permission. All rights reserved.

Scripture quotations marked TPT are from The Passion Translation®. Copyright © 2017, 2018, 2020 by Passion & Fire Ministries, Inc. Used by permission. All rights reserved. ThePassionTranslation.com.

Scripture quotations marked AMP are taken from The AMPLIFIED Bible, Copyright © 1954, 1958, 1962, 1964, 1965, 1987, 2015 by The Lockman Foundation. All rights reserved. Used by permission. (www.Lockman.org)

Cover design by Barbara De Simon Creative Business Solutions
Photo by Lance Reis on Unsplash
ISBN: 978-1-7383840-1-3

Spiritual Protection and Deliverance for our Children

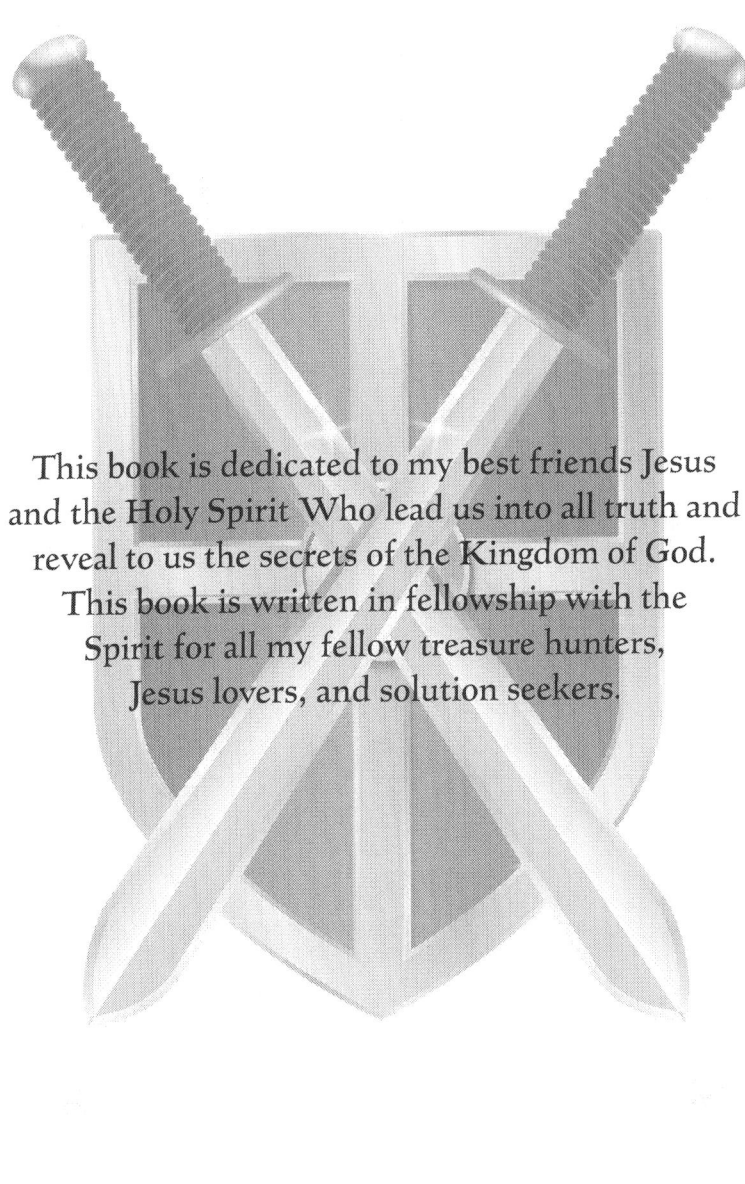

This book is dedicated to my best friends Jesus and the Holy Spirit Who lead us into all truth and reveal to us the secrets of the Kingdom of God. This book is written in fellowship with the Spirit for all my fellow treasure hunters, Jesus lovers, and solution seekers.

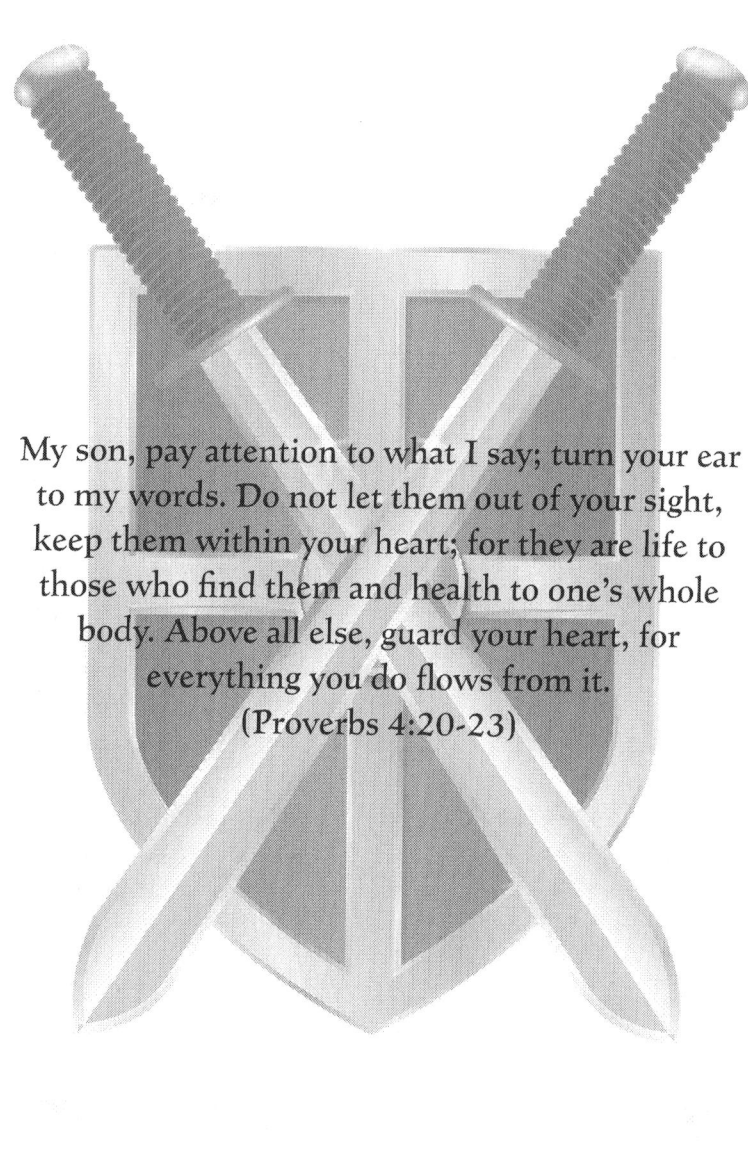

My son, pay attention to what I say; turn your ear to my words. Do not let them out of your sight, keep them within your heart; for they are life to those who find them and health to one's whole body. Above all else, guard your heart, for everything you do flows from it.
(Proverbs 4:20-23)

TABLE OF CONTENTS

TESTIMONIAL ———————————————————————— 1
PREFACE ———————————————————————————— 13

WHAT'S GOING ON WITH OUR KIDS?

INTRODUCTION ——————————————————————— 25
AUTHORITY —————————————————————————— 34

FOUNDATIONAL KNOWLEDGE TO BUILD ON

WHO'S WHO ——————————————————————————— 47
   Who is God? ———————————————————————— 47
   Who is Satan? ——————————————————————— 49
   Who Are You? ——————————————————————— 53
SPIRITUAL PROTECTION ———————————————— 63
DELIVERANCE: WHAT IS IT? ——————————— 77
   Who is Deliverance For? ———————————— 90
FAST TRACK TO TROUBLE ———————————————— 93
   How do we become demonized? ————————— 93
   What makes a religion a cult? ———————— 99
   Signs of Oppression —————————————————— 101

PREPARING YOURSELF TO STAND

PREPARING YOUR SPIRIT ———————————————— 107
PREPARING YOUR HEART ———————————————— 118
CLEANSING YOUR SPIRITUAL HOUSE ——————— 140
   The Orphan Spirit ——————————————————— 141
   Shame ——————————————————————————————— 142
   Rejection ——————————————————————————— 148
   Anger and Frustration with Our Kids ——— 150
   Unmet Expectations ———————————————————— 151
   Words and Curses ——————————————————————— 153
   Involvement in the Occult and Yoga ——— 155
   Sexual Sin —————————————————————————— 159
   Soul Ties ———————————————————————————— 161
UNITED WE STAND ———————————————————— 166

    The Resolution for Men 168
    The Resolution for Women 179
ELIMINATING FEAR 188
    Fear of Poverty 189
    Fear of Homosexuality in Your Children 194
    Fear of Suicide 198

STANDING FOR YOUR FAMILY

KINGS AND PRIESTS 207
    Your Idols 214
    Your Children's Idols 217
    Further Action 222
SPIRITS, ACCESS POINTS & SYMPTOMS 227
    Root Spirit of Antichrist 228
    Root Spirit of Fear 229
    Root Spirit of Bondage 231
    Deaf & Dumb Root Spirit 231
    Root Spirit of Hautiness/Pride 232
    Root Spirit of Stupor/Slumber 233
    Root Spirit of Jealousy 234
    Root Spirit of Heaviness 235
    Root Spirit of Harlotry/Prostitution 235
    Root Spirit of Lying 236
    Root Spirit of Death 237
    Root Spirit of Infirmity 238
    Root Spirit of Perversity 239
    Root Spirit of Divination 240
    Root Spirit of Error 241
    Final Prayer 241
FOLLOW THROUGH 252
CONCLUSION 256
NOTE FROM THE AUTHOR 261
ABOUT THE AUTHOR 263
APPENDIX A 265
REFERENCES 270
ENDNOTES 271

PREFACE

"What in the world is going on with our kids?" swirled through my mind as I heard heart wrenching stories from beautiful but desperate moms in our ladies' small group; compassion and empathy stirred in my heart fiercely. It could not be ignored. Never in my wildest imagination would I have thought children would be so difficult to manage and parenting would be so painful and challenging—even to the point of emotional and mental breakdown.

I have raised four children who are now all adults in their twenties, and never did any of them ever destroy their bedroom in a fit of rage or throw a piece of furniture across the room, or sucker-punch me in the gut. I don't say that to gloat or pat myself on the back, but I say that to emphasize the point that we are in an unprecedented, chaotic time in this world for many reasons. The dysfunction, perversion, and complete lack of boundaries is taking its toll on children, and something's got to change. Someone has got to step in and emphatically say, "not on my watch," and come along side parents to help them get to the root of the problem. If we don't start to do something different now, we're going to end up having to convert entire hospital buildings to psych wards with thousands committed.

Perhaps you have done all the things for your children—discipline, medical diagnosis, medication, therapy, counselling and its still not enough to temper their tantrums nor ease their anxiety. Perhaps you're at your wits end and you're at a loss of what to do next. Perhaps, even though you're exhausted, all the things aren't making enough of a difference. And perhaps you've cried out to God in prayer for a solution. My friend, I believe with all my heart this book may be the answer to your prayer.

Before I say more, let me pray for you and invite the Spirit of the Living God into this experience. Let's invite the Spirit of Life to breathe on us and these pages. Will you agree with me and receive from the Lord? Read through this prayer slowly and really hear what is being said and feel what the Spirit is getting ready to do on your behalf. Join me as I speak to God, interceding for you and your family:

> "Heavenly Father, thank You that You are good, and that Your mercies are new every morning, enduring forever! Thank You, God, that You are the God of breakthrough, and You have the answer for every problem. You are the Solution Bringer—the Problem Solver, the Life Giver every time, all the time. Nothing is beyond Your power, mercy, and love. Nothing is beyond Your reach. I put my hope in You God to release to every reader what they need—practical solutions, authority, power, and supernatural assistance in their mind, in their heart, their spirit and in their natural circumstances. Help each reader, Lord, to hear Your voice and receive Your wisdom on how to move forward naturally and spiritually.
>
> And Lord, I lift up every child represented by the parents who are reading this right now. I ask You, God, to intervene in their nervous system and bring them back to homeostasis, out of the *fight or flight* response and God, I ask You to heal the

neuropathways in their brain that have been created by fear, trauma, violence, anger, confusion, and depression. Would You fill in those pathways by Your mercy and grace and begin to give them thoughts of peace and safety in You. Begin to cause new healthy neuropathways, Lord, that will foster healthy responses and reactions. I speak "peace be still" to each of their senses, natural and spiritual. I say hyper-responsiveness in every sense—hearing, seeing, touching, smelling, tasting—come into divine order and alignment, RIGHT NOW, in Jesus' MIGHTY name. Lord, I stand in the gap for every parent reading this and every child they represent, and I confess every deep emotional connection, reliance and tie made with the wrong things—things they were never meant to rely on nor get emotional fuel from—like games, videos, and their characters, and I repent. I renounce and break every emotional tie and reliance on these things now in Jesus' name. I take authority over every spirit of confusion, chaos, and fear and I bind them; I break their power now! I command confusion, chaos, and fear to cease and desist right now, in Jesus' name. I speak healing and a new freedom over each child represented. Open a window of heaven over them now, God. Thank you, Lord. Thank You, Father. In Jesus' name, Amen."

Now I will exercise the authority Jesus has given me and I will speak over you:

I speak an end to everything in your heart that leads to death, right now. Despair, go! Discouragement, go! Hopelessness, go! Weariness, go! Hope deferred, go! I command faith to arise, now, in Jesus' name. I command faith to arise again, afresh, right now.

Beloved, you thought you'd have breakthrough by now, but you don't. Be brave, beloved. Be courageous! Pick up that hope again; it doesn't belong on the shelf. Hope belongs in your heart, and it needs to be placed in Jesus, and Jesus alone.

I speak fresh breath and new life into your heart and each of your spiritual senses right now and I say, "Be open, now," in Jesus' name. Receive hope afresh now. Receive new strength, new vision and new hearing now, in Jesus' mighty name. Amen.

Take a deep breath and just sit in that for a moment. Continue to breathe deep and slow, focusing your mind on Jesus. Allow the Lord to do what He wants to do in this moment. Let Him bring a release and a refreshing now.

Wrestle through your thoughts and bring every thought that is disobedient to God and His power and mercy into subjection. All things are possible to those who believe. Yes! I said, ALL things are possible to those who believe. That's you. I know, you think you've tried everything, but you actually haven't. Not everything. I know this because your situation is still not well, and it is God's will for you and your family to live in peace. Jesus died for it.

What you read in the above declaration and prayer may be new to you; that's okay. Just because it's new, doesn't mean it's wrong. Take dominion over every argument that raises itself up against the knowledge of God; tear them down with violence (2 Cor. 10:4-5). Do not allow arguments and dissension to steal from you right now. Instead, engage your spirit to sense the presence of the Holy Spirit right here—right where you are.

Go back and read through the italicized statements again if you struggled to receive. Engage your heart with it and allow it to do its work. Holy Spirit, come! Minister through these words.

Okay, if you're settled, let's continue.

As you begin this book, would you be willing to push the reset button on your faith and hope? Would you be willing to put ALL your hope in God rather than all the other things? Rather than the world? Even the doctors, for now? I'm not saying stop going to the doctor, but at least stop putting all your hope in him/her. And realize that God is your hope. And He never fails.

Perhaps that's new to you. Perhaps this already seems a bit too spiritual and you're not sure if you want to go that deep. My friend, when something you're doing is not working, you need to try something different. Your life and the lives of your children are at stake. Surface faith is not working; you need to go deep to get the answers that will rescue your family. Jesus wants you to come into the deep places with Him—deep into His heart, His mercy, and His wisdom.

It's time to meet the *powerful now* Jesus—the Jesus Who is real, present, and ALIVE and is wanting to meet your need NOW. We don't have to wait until we cross over into heaven to be with Jesus. He is here with us right now in Spirit, waiting for us to receive Him into our circumstances and home.

Open your heart, friend. Receive Him and receive new possibilities. Receive new hope only found in the person of Jesus.

Okay, let's go. Let's dive in and let breakthrough begin!

I recently experienced a full-circle moment with God as He reconfirmed my calling and brought me back to interceding for children and families. I typed wildly on my computer as the Lord downloaded prayers for friends I would visit that evening—prayers that were targeted toward the spiritual warfare surrounding their family. For years, my ministry centered around warring for families, mostly regarding fertility struggles, *until* I wrote my first book in 2016 called *Barren No More*, and then my second in 2018 called *Key to Fertility*. I thought I had completed my assignment for families, but now suddenly my heart was burning once again, not for infertility but for the protection and deliverance of our young. I found myself once again called into battle for children as the door of ministry flew wide open, pulling me in.

I shouldn't be surprised. Back in 2013 or so, the Lord told me about the battle for our children that would ramp up in the years to come. Even before I began to write books, the Lord had me making baby blankets with the Priestly blessing embroidered on them, interceding for those trying to conceive, and telling everyone in my sphere of influence to declare the blessing found in Numbers 6:24-26[1] over their babies and children every night.

I remember one night vividly; my eyes shot open at 3AM as God's presence filled my room. The Spirit reminded me of Moses as I saw in my mind's eye a bush on fire yet unconsumed and the Lord said to me, "I have heard the cries of my people." I knew in my spirit that He meant those who were trying to conceive. The Lord then said, "Go! Go and set my people free."

The next morning, I stood in front of the mirror getting ready for the day, and I asked God directly, "What is happening right now that you have me doing all these things with the blankets, blogging, and interceding for families? And almost as clear as I could hear my own voice, I *immediately* heard the Spirit say, "In the last days I will pour out my Spirit on all flesh. Your *sons* and *daughters* will prophesy..." (Joel 2:28 paraphrased) and suddenly I knew. Suddenly I knew that we were in a battle for our children because the devil does not want our children to prophesy. Accurate prophetic utterances from children will be a catalyst to the end-time harvest and the enemy knows it.

I continued blogging and warning parents. I told them what the Lord told me, "Declare the blessing from Numbers six over your children and as you do, walls of protection around them will be built." He even gave me a scripture to confirm, that blessing and being surrounded with protection (or being hedged in) were connected. In Job 1:10, Satan says to God referring to Job, "Have you not put a *hedge (of protection)* around him and his household and everything he has? You have *blessed* the work of his hands, so that his flock and herds are spread throughout the land" (NIV, brackets and italics added).

Out of these revelations I began writing the first two books connected to warring for families. And now here I am again with families and their young children on my heart. Only this time, the mama bear in me is rising, taking a much bolder stance because now the enemy is causing children to suffer, and I will not just stand by and say nothing. Not on my watch!

What I am about to write will not be accepted by everyone, but that is okay. I am not looking for popularity or to be liked. I am looking to co-labor with the Holy Spirit and save those who are in pits of despair, depression, fear, and the like, not knowing how to get out. I am looking to reach out a hand for parents to grab hold of so they can find peace again and a sense of normalcy in a messy and confused world.

So, buckle up my friend! Put your humility on and open your mind to God's solutions to your parenting predicament. It may not be anything you've heard before, but it's real, it's raw and it is divine power ready to bust through everything that resists what is holy and true.

I stand in the authority of Jesus Christ, and I intercede on your behalf commanding freedom to come and sanity to return to your family, in Jesus' name! The Lord your God has NOT given you a spirit of fear, but of power, love, discipline and a sound mind (see 2 Timothy 1:7).

This book will proceed in four sections. In the first section we will identify the problem. In the second section we will lay a foundation of knowledge needed to move forward. In the third section we will prepare you to stand against the enemy on your child's (children's) behalf, and in the fourth section, we will get into solutions and the prayers needed to activate healing in your children.

Get your highlighter out and your pen to make notes as the Lord shows you what applies to your individual situations.

The Lord says, "Enough is enough! Line up with Me. Line up with My plumb line—that which is straight right and true—in every area of your life. Eliminate everything that competes with righteousness, faithfulness and My goodness and you will be healed. What has been tipsy turvy and upside down will be made right again. Get ready for My power to flow through you as you take your stand with Me."

Praise the Lord!

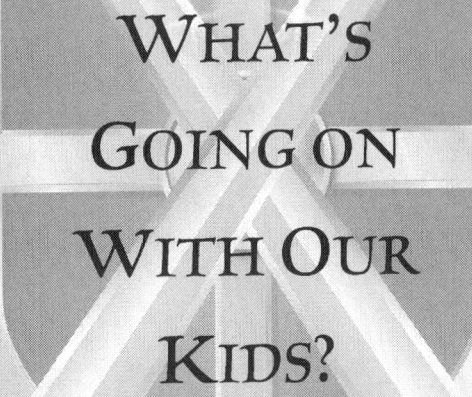

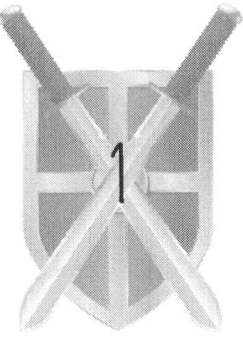

INTRODUCTION

This past week I had the privilege of coming along side a family who was struggling with the behaviors of one of their children. We talked about spiritual warfare strategies and pinpointed several opportunities the devil had over the last number of years to oppress their family. I taught them warfare prayer and how to close the doors that left them open to the enemy's influence and as they applied what I had taught them, amazing results followed.

This beautiful family was so open to learn and hear about the realities of spiritual warfare and how it applied to them and their children. They were also so eager to apply everything they learned. What a blessing! Their obedience was rewarded as the Lord came through on their behalf changing the atmosphere in their home, changing their hearts toward one another and laying an axe to the root of their child's defiant behaviors.

In just two weeks, they went from a full psychological evaluation being eminent, to normal life, not perfect, but normal life with young children simply learning how to manage their emotions and fleshly desires. What an honor to be used of the Lord in this way. I became so fired up with the results that I decided more families need to have this information available to them. I can't sit in everyone's living room in person, but I can write this book for people to read. So, I take this bold step in faith, believing that many families will benefit from it.

Why do I say "bold" step? Well, deliverance has been a controversial topic, even in the church, and no one really wants to talk about it despite the fact that it was a normal occurrence in the Bible and done out in the open—even in the streets. We see Jesus and the Apostles delivering people in many instances. Paul delivers a servant girl from a spirit of divination in Acts 16:16-18; she had been following the apostles around loudly announcing to *everyone* who they were and why they were there which would have drawn unnecessary attention to them, possibly putting them in harms way.

Jesus delivered many.[2] We see one example in Luke 13:11-16. A woman who was completely bent over because of a spirit of infirmity in her body, was completely healed and delivered through a word from Jesus, "Woman, you are set free from your infirmity" (v.12 NIV). The Bible says, "Then he put his hands on her, and immediately she straightened up and praised God" (v.13 NIV).

In Mark 7 we hear of a Greek woman whose *little daughter* had an unclean spirit, coming to Jesus and begging Him to heal her. We don't know how the demon was affecting the child specifically, only that it was severe. Originally Jesus wasn't going to help her because she was a Gentile, but His compassion shifted in her favor according to the mother's faith. Jesus said to her in Mark 7:29, "For such a reply, you may go; the demon has left your daughter" (NIV). The young child wasn't even there with them, but at home. Despite that, Jesus delivered the child from the demon with a word as He operated in the Spirit realm... where time and distance have no influence.

We see in numerous instances in the Bible that deliverance was needed by many. The devil and demons are still in this world today and we still need to resist them and cast them out, just like they used to. First Peter 5:8-9a says, "Be sober, be vigilant; because your adversary the devil walks about like a roaring lion, seeking whom he may devour. Resist him, steadfast in the faith..." (NKJV).

It's time to war for our children. Yes, there is an invisible spiritual battle happening right now behind the scenes of our lives. The battle has been raging for a while now and if you have been aware of it, you're probably already engaged in it. Unfortunately, though, many have been ignorant of it—even those who are in the church. For instance, many have had no idea that games, toys, and media on all fronts have been and are being used by the enemy to completely highjack our children.

With the launch of the World Wide Web in 1991, but more so with the launch of the first iPhone and iPad in 2007 and 2010 respectively, came the dawn of a brand-new parenting era. It was something no one understood or was ready for. Suddenly the world, and ALL its information and images, were at the fingertips of anyone with a device—even young children. The iPad became the favorite babysitter for stressed-out parents who just needed to keep their toddler happy and quiet for a time so they could get other things done or have time to themselves. It felt like a Godsend, but little did they know the addictive power of the screen and the games created to capture the minds of children. The enemy of our soul, Satan, knew exactly what he was secretly accomplishing through the creative minds designing the new era media.

So as not to vilify *every* person creating media, some of the creators weren't aware of the sinister scheme of the enemy to reinforce the kingdom of darkness through games, movies, and videos. Even so, some were and are, and some are even now partnering with the kingdom of darkness purposely to accomplish Satan's purposes. It absolutely breaks my heart to know this; we need to be aware of the schemes of the enemy, so he does not outwit us (2 Cor. 2:11 NIV). Lord, have mercy! Rescue and save those entrapped by lies and the darkness so prevalent in the world today.

The scariest part is that the kingdom of darkness is seen as *cool*. It is seen as cool and exciting to be entertained by and to engage with, evil forces. Sadly, those in search of an immediate *rush* or *thrill* of some kind will do just about anything to get it but they end up suffering in the long run because of it. They don't know about unseen but *very real* demons in the heavenly realm that entrap them as they choose to feed their soul violence, fighting, murder, fear, and terror through media and electronics. They are completely ignorant of the long-term consequences of such activity because they're either not aware of or they don't believe in demons.

Despite what people believe, demons are very real! And demons love it when people don't believe in them; this gives them innumerable opportunities to oppress their victims. They want us to stay ignorant and uneducated so they can cause chaos in our lives.

As we begin this book, here's some key scriptures straight from the Bible that tell us we are in a real battle:

> Finally, my brethren, be strong in the Lord and in the power of His might. Put on the whole armor of God, that you may be able to stand against the wiles of the devil. For we do not wrestle against flesh and blood, but against principalities, against powers, against the rulers of the darkness of this age, against spiritual *hosts* of wickedness in the heavenly *places*. Therefore take up the whole armor of God, that you may be able to withstand in the evil day, and having done all, to stand (Ephesians 6:10-13 NKJV).

We see from Ephesians 6 that we *are* in a battle, and we battle against principalities, powers, rulers of the darkness and against spiritual hosts of wickedness in heavenly places. All these descriptions are speaking of demons—demons that are ranked according to power and authority. Don't let this discourage you though friend, we are equipped by Jesus to stand in His authority to resist these foes. Keep reading and you will be equipped with the truth you need.

Ephesians goes on after verse thirteen to tell us about each piece of armor God has given us and what it is for. We will go into more detail about these things in chapter seven.

Another scripture tells us about our spiritual weapons:

> For though we walk in the flesh, we do not war according to the flesh. For the weapons of our warfare are not carnal but mighty in God for pulling down strongholds, casting down arguments and every high thing that exalts itself against the knowledge of God, bringing every thought into captivity to the obedience of Christ, and being ready to punish all disobedience when your obedience is fulfilled (2 Corinthians 10:3-6 NKJV).

This scripture is part of Paul's defense of his ministry to the Corinthians and he was confronting some in the Corinthian church who didn't believe that the apostles were operating by the wisdom and power of the Holy Spirit (see verse 2). They mistakenly believed that the apostles were operating according to the flesh. Paul boldly told them of the spiritual weapons they (the apostles) had been given according to the Spirit of God. Christians who walk in maturity also have access to these weapons, as they are weapons available to those who walk by the Spirit.

Just as a side note, you may be wondering about the end of verse six that says, "and being ready to punish all disobedience when your obedience is fulfilled." Reading through the following chapters of 2 Corinthians, we see that Paul calls out a group in the church that continue to sin in the same way over and over (see 2 Cor. 13:1-4 MSG) and it is this group that Paul is speaking about in verse six of chapter ten. He confirms to the Corinthian church that they (the Apostles) were ready to discipline all individuals who continued to sin even after the church, as a corporate body, had agreed to come into obedience and alignment with Christ and the Apostles, respectively. Each member of the church was expected to walk in humility and holiness by the power of the Holy Spirit within them—a teaching that seems to be missing in many westernized churches.

Lastly, Matthew 16:19 is another verse that gives us keys to spiritual warfare. It says:

> I will give you the keys (authority) of the kingdom of heaven; and whatever you bind [forbid, declare to be improper and unlawful] on earth will have [already] been bound in heaven, and whatever you loose [permit, declare lawful] on earth will have [already] been loosed in heaven (AMP).

Jesus was telling Peter, that whatever Peter declared unlawful or bound would be bound (constrained) in the spiritual realm and whatever he (Peter) declared lawful or loosed would be loosed in the spiritual realm. So, Jesus was telling Peter that He was giving the church authority over how the spirits, angels and demons, affect the atmosphere and earthly realm. You as part of the church, hidden in Christ, have that same authority[3] as you overcome in your own life and work out your salvation, or walk in victory over temptations, ungodly heart attitudes and the demonic realm.

We indeed have spiritual weapons to wage war, and we have the armor of God to protect us as we fight. Fighting this battle looks more like praying fervently, binding and loosing, and decreeing the Word of God than swinging a physical sword. It looks like standing our ground and taking authority over the spiritual atmosphere and any demons that may be coming against us. It also looks like repenting for how we have cooperated with demons in the past and getting free from their bondage.

Yes, Christ has already conquered the demonic realm (Col. 2:15), and we already have victory in Christ, but we must *enforce* that victory here on the earth because the enemy and his cohorts are liars, deceivers, and opportunists. If we give them an inch of agreement, they will take a mile and make our lives miserable. They will take advantage of any opportunity and weasel their way into our psyche, thoughts, and behaviors.

Take note! We are not fighting *for* victory; we are fighting *from* the victory that Christ has already won on our behalf. James 4:7 specifically tells us to submit to God and "resist the devil." When we resist the devil, he will flee but we can't skip over that step. Resistance is necessary to be free from the enemy's influence. And it's not just about resisting temptation to sin but resisting the lies he plants in our mind, as well as the confusion, the chaos, and the demons that try to get us all worked up, anxious, frustrated, offended and angry.

We are indeed in a spiritual battle in our own lives and for our children. This book is intended to discuss how we get into trouble as individuals, parents, and families by giving the enemy a foothold, how to recover from those challenges using Godly wisdom and the spiritual weapons we've been given, and how to prevent those challenges in the first place.

Welcome to *Spiritual Protection and Deliverance for Our Children*. If you've picked up this book, you may be looking for an answer to the question, "Why is my child behaving this way and what do I do about it?" If so, you've come to the right place.

Although my goal is not to give advice on discipline or behavior management techniques, you *will* find some scattered throughout these pages. Take them or leave them—your choice. However, there are many informative books already available from child psychologists and others regarding this topic. For example, *You Can't Make Me (But I Can Be Persuaded): Strategies for Bringing Out the Best in Your Strong-Willed Child* by Cynthia Ulrich Tobias looks like a great book, offering solid behavior management tools.

My goal with this book is to offer a solution for Christian families that when applied in faith, addresses the *possible root-causes* to a child's persistent, defiant, and angry behavior that goes beyond normal childhood shenanigans. Of course, I *cannot* guarantee anything, as your results are directly related to your response—your willingness to be resolute, to stand in your authority in Christ, to align your life, actions and attitudes to the *full* counsel of scripture, to move in active faith and humility, and to believe the Word of God with all your heart. Your results also depend on your willingness to thoroughly purge your own heart as you are led through each chapter. There are no shortcuts. (In fact, short cuts may be dangerous, so please don't skip over anything.) I will do my very best to guide you along the way and give you the information you need to move forward.

Let's begin.

AUTHORITY

I think the most important and foundational topic we can discuss in this book relating to spiritual protection and deliverance for our children is authority. In this chapter, we will talk about how it operates in the natural world and how it relates to parenting.

Authority. What is it? Who has it or who *should* have it? Who do we *perceive* as having it? And how has this changed over the years?

According to Oxford languages, authority is *the power or right to give orders, make decisions and enforce obedience.* Merriam-Webster says authority is *the power to influence or command thought, opinion, or behavior.* Cambridge dictionary says authority is *the moral or legal right or ability to control.* Out of these definitions we see common threads of power and the right or ability to use that power. The purpose of authority is to strongly influence or exercise some level of control over thought and/or behavior.

Who Has Authority?

God has authority. The government on all levels has authority as well as the governing bodies they appoint or create to lead in different areas like health, immigration, security, travel etc. Some people like doctors, lawyers, and judges have authority in their area of expertise because they have chosen to take on that responsibility and they are educated to do so. Police have authority. Teachers have authority in their classroom and parents have authority in their home and over their children. Very often the level of authority someone has is directly related to the responsibility they are given, take, or hold. In the case of a parent for instance, they have authority over their children simply because the parent has either birthed them or adopted them and are responsible for their care and well-being. Perhaps you can think of others who have authority but for our purposes right now, it's not necessary to list them all.

Who do You Perceive as Having Authority?

It's interesting that our perception of who's in authority (in our lives) can be different from what I've listed above. For instance, perhaps some don't see the government as having complete authority over them—that is until they don't file their tax return, or they're caught not complying to government-imposed restrictions. Sometimes we don't like it, and there may be times we take a risk and don't comply, but the government in fact does have authority over us because if we're caught, there are consequences. Some don't perceive doctors as having authority *over them* because their own personal autonomy is of greater importance; they choose not to submit to the doctor's orders or advice. Sometimes that works out for them and other times it doesn't.

Who do you, as an adult, see as having authority over you? I'll go first. Number one, of course, God. God, Jesus and the Holy Spirit have ALL authority over me and my life, and I submit to His authority every moment of every day (sometimes not perfectly) in all the matters that I clearly know His direction. The leadership at my church, I see as having authority over me and it is Godly for me to submit to them as best I can, *as far as* they submit to the Lord. And of course, the police have authority over me. Lastly, the government. I don't always agree with them, which is why I exercise my right to vote and pray for them. It's possible there will be a time when I refuse to submit to their leadership, but that I leave in God's hands for now. I will always be loyal to Christ first and foremost.

When I was a child, it was a little different. I grew up in the 70's and 80's so in addition to all the above, my teachers and *every* staff member at the school had authority over me and they did not hesitate to *exercise* that authority. I even remember, very early on, that in persistent cases of disobedience, corporal punishment was used. I did not experience *that* at school, but I *knew* not to get myself sent to the principal's office.

Additionally, my parents, grandparents and all those who were considered my "elders" also had authority over me, and I submitted to them... most of the time. When I didn't, I felt the consequences. I remember we had a neighbor that lived on the corner and if I so much as put a toe on his lawn, he yelled at me. I learned quickly to stay off his grass!

What Has Changed?

Over the years, since I was a child, much has changed and is still changing. In many respects, that change has been good as there were many school officials and others who abused their power, not exercising their authority with love, kindness nor wisdom. I, myself, can attest to that with 100% accuracy as I was one of those children who was mistreated, all in the name of discipline.

Unfortunately, I believe that in an effort to not make the same mistakes our parents made, we may have *over-corrected* ourselves, causing the pendulum to swing way too far to the other side, so much so that we barely even see ourselves as having authority over our children anymore. Some prefer to think of themselves as their children's friend rather than their parent, but the purpose of the authoritarian structure of family is to maintain order and a sense of safety for children. In fact, when parents cease to exercise clear authority in their family, mayhem results.

AUTHORITY STRUCTURES ARE IN PLACE TO MAINTAIN ORDER AND PROVIDE SAFETY.

There was a study conducted by a group of landscape architects whereby they studied the behavioral differences of children playing on a playground with and without a fence surrounding it. They found that the children on the playground without the fence huddled around the teachers, refusing to explore any further. On the contrary, the children who played on the playground *with* the fence enjoyed the entire playground and explored the space more freely as they knew where the boundaries were.[4]

Boundaries communicate safety and when parents don't clearly identify boundaries through rules, authority, and appropriate discipline, children will flounder, be anxious, clingy, and purposefully misbehave in an effort to identify limits so they feel safe.

New York Times bestselling author and Psychologist, Dr. James Dobson, has some interesting comments about children challenging authority and needing to establish clear social order in his book, *Temper Your Child's Tantrums*. He says, "Why are children so pugnacious?" Yes, I had to look that word up. According to Oxford Languages, *pugnacious* means *eager or quick to argue, quarrel, or fight*. Dobson goes on to say:

> "Everyone knows that they (children) are lovers of justice and law and order and secure boundaries... Why, then, can't parents resolve all conflicts by the use of quiet discussions and explanations and gentle pats on the head?
>
> The answer is found in the curious value system of children that respects strength and courage (when combined with love) . . . You see, boys and girls care about the issue of "who's toughest." Whenever a youngster moves into a new neighborhood or a new school district, he usually has to fight (either verbally or physically) to establish himself in the hierarchy of strength. Anyone who understands

children knows that there is a "top dog" in every group, and there is a poor little defeated pup at the bottom of the heap. And every child between those extremes knows where he stands in relation to the others."[5]

I don't know about you, but that hits deep. Perhaps you too remember the school yard struggles that determined your place in the group all those years ago. And perhaps you see your own children going through similar things now.

This dynamic of social hierarchy plays out at home too as children pull their parents into a battle of the wills with directly defiant behavior. You know the challenge well. We're not talking about spilling the milk or forgetting to pick up toys. We're talking about when a child purposefully goes against the will of the parent just to see what he/she will do. They really just want reassurance of who's in charge—who's the *top dog*. Just like a night security guard will test a door that should be locked by trying to open it, a child is greatly reassured that they are protected and safe within definitive boundaries as they test their parents' authority and confidence in it. It is vital that parents meet the challenge head on and *win* the altercation the *very first time* defiant behavior occurs. It could come as early as eighteen months of age.

I remember it vividly with our first-born. It was her second birthday, and she was purposely pushing papers onto the floor from the coffee table, making a mess. I told her very firmly, "No!" as I picked the papers up off the floor and put them back on the table. She looked at the papers and then looked at me and I again, while having eye contact with her told her, "No." But after hearing me, she continued looking at me, put her hand on the paper and without breaking eye contact, shoved the paper to the floor again. Now, in the grand scheme of things, it wasn't a big deal. It was just a few papers on the floor. Right? Well, what made it a big deal was she purposely defied me just to see what I would do.

These are the moments when our **very next** move speaks louder than any words. We must communicate with clarity, peace, and confidence that we are in charge and outright defiance will **not** be tolerated. How you choose to do that is your choice, but make sure your response is appropriate to your child's age and temperament. Personally, I have found that for a child between fifteen and twenty-four months, *one controlled* spank to a *bare* bottom, *directly* after the defiance is most effective. You are welcome to disagree with me, but it worked extremely well for us. I only spanked our oldest twice, and our second-born once. The youngest two were not spanked at all because they were never defiant. Outright defiance is the *only* time a spank should be administered, in my opinion, and I would NOT advise giving a spank to a child over the age of three. If defiance has not been dealt with by that time, another form of discipline should be used.

If we are willing to take defiant behavior seriously and establish our authority in the home early, we will have it easier later when they're older. *Make sure you do not let defiant behavior slide.* Confront it *each and every time* as it comes and make sure you win. After a few times, children will learn who's in charge, and they will respect your authority.

Unfortunately, if you don't win the *initial* battle of the wills, you will struggle with disrespect in your relationship with your child, until you do win *consistently*. And that could be a very exhausting process. All hope is not lost though. There is good news. By the end of this book, you will have some tools and strategies to help you break any negative patterns that might be occurring in your relationship with your child. So, hang in there!

The godly authority that the Lord has given to parents over their own children has been under attack. Underneath it all, I believe it is Satan's agenda to strip parents of their authority so he can gain control of children. Unfortunately, he is successfully doing it as laws are now being passed that give the public school system authority to assist children in gender reassignment, birth-control, abortion, and all kinds of other medical matters without the parents' knowledge or consent. Parents are no longer privy to what their children are doing at school or learning. Sadly, the government and schools are attempting to replace the parent, and I vehemently encourage all parents to do whatever it takes to regain their role as the authority in their children's lives, even if it means pulling them out of school and homeschooling. Parents are supposed to be the gate keepers of their home—the protectors of it, and they do that through maintaining and exercising authority.

If you have been hurt by strict authoritarian parents who did not know how to parent with mercy or grace, I am so sorry. If this experience has caused you to think that you could raise children without exercising authority, I am sorry you were deceived into thinking that. There is a balance that we need to achieve between being the authority in our home and exercising it with kindness, grace and understanding—most definitely. It's vital that we connect with our children on a heart level and understand that behaviors communicate need and the best way to manage behaviors is to meet the underlying need causing the behavior. It's not rocket science! Right? But somehow, our parents missed the memo—at least mine did. They cared more about controlling me than understanding and meeting my emotional needs for connection.

Children act out because they are any one or more of the following at any given time: scared, tired, hungry, in pain, over-stimulated, bored, not feeling loved, angry, triggered (reminded of something traumatic that happened in the past), feeling rejected, not certain they are safe because parents have not stood in authority proving they can be trusted, addicted or oppressed by demons. And yes, mental health problems can be caused by brain chemistry being out of wack, but I believe, more often there is an emotional and spiritual struggle not recognized or addressed.

If you can't get to the root of a behavior by talking to your child about it, pray. Ask the Lord what is going on. In prayer, think through what happened right before the behavior began and perhaps the Holy Spirit will reveal something. By all means though, make sure you communicate love, concern and care to your child, no matter what. A heart-to-heart connection is your number one priority.

If there are extremely violent and defiant behaviors happening, there is a very high probability you are dealing with demonization—not possession, but oppression. Not to worry though! It can be dealt with in love and without getting weird, so keep reading my friend. Everything you need is found in these pages.

Lastly, we do need to take into consideration that society is removing boundaries in all kinds of areas. Children are being taught that they can be any gender they want. We know there are only two genders, as the Lord made male and female, but the world has gone crazy with it. Children are also being given sexual knowledge way before they are capable of carrying the weight of it. There are so many options and choices and decisions that children are expected to make. It's completely overwhelming for them. It seems that children simply can't be children anymore; the years of innocence have been stolen.

Your job as a parent is to intervene and advocate for them. If you must remove the internet from your home to protect your children, do it. Get rid of games, movies, videos, devices, whatever is causing an overload of information and activity in their mind.[1] Slow down as a family and unplug. Move out of the city if you must. Your family's wellbeing is your number one priority. Desperate times call for desperate measures.

Let's continue and learn more of how to partner with the Lord in bringing restoration to our families.

Are you with me?

---

[1] Before you throw out your child's favorite things, read through this whole book to get proper strategy in how to do this without traumatizing your children more. This is covered in chapter 12.

Foundational Knowledge To Build On

WHO'S WHO

This chapter right here is going to give you the most important truths you can use to enforce and defend the victory Christ has already won on your behalf. Get your highlighter out and ready to go! Let's consider who is who in this cosmic battle between good and evil.

Who is God?
God Almighty, Elohim, Jehovah, The Beginning and The End, The Great I Am, The Creator of all, He is supreme, rules over all and He is the most important, most powerful participant. He has always existed and is completely independent all on His own; He doesn't need anything or anyone although He loves us and created us to bring Him glory. Acts 17:24-25 says:

> God, who made the world and everything in it, since He is Lord of heaven and earth, does not dwell in temples made with hands. Nor is He worshipped with men's hands, as though He needed anything, since He gives to all life, breath, and all things (NKJV).

God is faithful and does not change in character or in His purposes; His character and His purposes remain the same. This means we can trust Him forever. James 1:17 says, "Every good gift and every perfect gift is from above, and comes down from the Father of lights, with whom there is no variation or shadow of turning (NKJV). Hebrews 13:8 says, "Jesus Christ is the same yesterday, today, and forever (NKJV). And we know that Jesus is the exact representation of the Father as Jesus said to Philip in John 14:9, "...Anyone who has seen me has seen the Father..." (NIV).

God is omnipresent—everywhere all the time, without size or spatial dimensions. God is omnipotent—all powerful and omniscient; He knows everything. God is preeminent, surpassing all others.

And my favorite: God is love and God is good, all the time. He is exceedingly merciful. First John 4:16 says, "And we have known and believed the love that God has for us. God is love, and he who abides in love abides in God, and God in him" (NKJV).

God is also just. He is a good and faithful judge. Here's Job 37:5-13 describing His great power over the earth:

> God thunders marvelously with His voice; He does great things which we cannot comprehend. For He says to the snow, 'Fall on the earth;' Likewise to the

gentle rain and the heavy rain of His strength. He seals the hand of every man, that all men may know His work. The beasts go into dens, and remain in their lairs. From the chamber *of the south* comes the whirlwind, And cold from the scattering winds *of the north*. By the breath of God ice is given, And the broad waters are frozen. Also with moisture He saturates the thick clouds; He scatters His bright clouds. And they swirl about, being turned by His guidance, that they may do whatever He commands them on the face of the whole earth. He causes it to come, whether for correction, or for His land, or for mercy" (NKJV).

God, Jesus and the Holy Spirit are all equal in their majesty and power. They differ in their function, but they are all in harmony and agreement with one another. Jesus and Holy Spirit submit completely to the Father and do His bidding perfectly.

Who is Satan?

Satan is a created being (created by God), a fallen angel who began as an archangel named Lucifer.

It's a very common mindset to think about God and Satan as being opposite one another—good and evil. But this mindset leads us to also think that God and Satan are equal in power, when they are emphatically not.

God is the Creator and Satan is the creation. No creation is ever greater or even equal to its creator—ever. In fact, the creation is always subject to its creator. Let's consider this by looking at Job 1:6-7:

> Now there was a day when the sons of God (angels) came to present themselves before the LORD, and Satan (adversary, accuser) also came among them. The LORD said to Satan, "From where have you come?" Then Satan answered the LORD, "From roaming around on the earth and from walking around on it" (AMP).

As we continue to read in Job, God asks Satan if he had considered Job—if he had noticed how upright Job is. God brags on Job as if to tempt Satan into sifting him. (When I first began reading the book of Job, I was a bit ticked at God for this but later in the book I began to understand that God had to deal with Job's pride.) Satan says to God:

> Does Job fear God for nothing? Have you not put a hedge around him and his household and everything he has? You have blessed the work of his hands, so that his flock and herds are spread throughout the land. But now stretch out your hand and strike everything he has, and he will surely curse you to your face (Job 1:9 NIV).

In verse twelve God responds, "Very well, then, everything he has is in your power, but on the man himself do not lay a finger" (Job 1:12 NIV). We see from this exchange that God holds the power, and Satan cannot do anything to Job without God's consent. In essence we see that God has Satan on a very short leash. The important takeaway from all this is even *before* Jesus overcame all demonic powers on our behalf at the cross, Satan could not just do whatever he wanted; he was subject to God.

It is suggested by some theologians that Lucifer was the leader of worship on the mountain of the Lord. Here's Ezekiel 28:12b-17 which describes who Satan was in heaven and his unfortunate rebellion:

> "You *were* the seal of perfection, full of wisdom and perfect in beauty. You were in Eden, the garden of God; every precious stone *was* your covering: the sardius, topaz, and diamond, beryl, onyx, and jasper, sapphire, turquoise, and emerald with gold. The workmanship of your timbrels and pipes was prepared for you on the day you were created. You *were* the anointed cherub who covers; I established you; you were on the holy mountain of God; you walked back and forth in the midst of fiery stones. You were perfect in your ways from the day you were created, till iniquity was found in you. "By the abundance of your trading you became filled with violence within, and you sinned; therefore I cast you as a profane thing out of the mountain of God; and I destroyed you, O covering cherub, from the midst of the fiery stones (NKJV).

Also, portions of Isaiah 14, which describes the king of Babylon, goes beyond describing an earthly king to describing the spiritual power behind that king—Satan himself:

> "How you are fallen from heaven, O Lucifer, son of the morning! *How* you are cut down to the ground, you who weakened the nations! For you have said in your heart: 'I will ascend into heaven, I will exalt my throne above the stars of God; I will also sit on the mount of the congregation on the farthest sides

of the north; I will ascend above the heights of the clouds, I will be like the Most High" (NKJV).

So, we know that Satan was kicked out of heaven and took a third of the angels with him (Revelation 12:4-9). In the New Testament, he is called "the god of this world" (2 Cor. 4:4), "the thief" (John 10:10), and the "father of lies." Jesus tells us about his nature in John 8:44:

> "You belong to your father, the devil, and you want to carry out your father's desires. He was a murderer from the beginning, not holding to the truth, for there is no truth in him. When he lies, he speaks his native language, for he is a liar and the father of lies" (NIV).

The good news in all of this is that Jesus took him on and overcame, disarming the enemy and all his minions, making a public spectacle of them all (Colossians 2:15). Jesus' crucifixion and resurrection stripped the devil of any authority he had to operate in power over us. Colossians says in the Amplified Bible:

> When you were dead in your sins and in the uncircumcision of your flesh (worldliness, manner of life), God made you alive together with Christ, having [freely] forgiven us all our sins, having canceled out the certificate of debt consisting of legal demands [which were in force] against us and which were hostile to us. And this certificate He has set aside *and* completely removed by nailing it to the cross. When He had disarmed the rulers and authorities [those supernatural forces of evil operating against us], He made a public example of

them [exhibiting them as captives in His triumphal procession], having triumphed over them through the cross" (Colossians 2:13-15 AMP).

Satan is the father of lies and he is an expert at deception. In fact, he acts much like one of those creatures on the earth that will puff themselves up to appear bigger than they really are to intimidate predators. He's a fake. His complete end is near. He is now and will always be the loser. And he knows it. He doesn't want you to know it... but now you do.

Please do not spend another moment intimidated by him. There is absolutely no reason for you to fear him. He is a bug under your feet, so let's stomp on him good.

Who Are You?

I'm going to warn you right now; this is going to seem like a trick question. Who are you? Think about that for a moment. How would you answer that question?

Most of us would answer that question with what we do—our occupation, what roles we fill and perhaps how many children we have, but that's not really *who* we are at our core. In fact, if we define ourselves by our occupation and roles, our identity becomes muddled and we become uncertain of who we are when we perhaps lose our job, change careers and/or when our roles in life shift, for instance when our children grow up, start their own lives and become independent. It *can* cause mothers especially to go through an identity crisis when they are no longer needed by their children. It is much better to define ourselves by what won't change— by the eternal aspects of who we are. With that in mind,

I might answer, "I am Barbara Jane, daughter of the most-high God, Jehovah, younger sibling to Jesus Christ of Nazareth, blessed and highly favored, called to encourage the Bride of Christ to walk in everything Christ died to give her—freedom, righteousness, and holiness. All who have surrendered their hearts to Jesus and accepted God's free gift of salvation can also claim their identity as a son or daughter of God. John 1:10-13 says:

> He was in the world, and the world was made through Him, and the world did not know Him. He came to His own, and His own did not receive Him. But as many as received Him, to them He gave the right to become children of God, to those who believe in His name: who were born, not of blood, nor of the will of the flesh, nor of the will of man, but of God" (NKJV).

As children of God, we have been re-born—born of the Spirit. In John 3, Nicodemus, a Pharisee, meets with Jesus in secret and tries to understand how one can be *born again*. Beginning in verse five, Jesus says to Nicodemus:

> Most assuredly, I say to you, unless one is born of water and the Spirit, he cannot enter the kingdom of God. That which is born of the flesh is flesh, and that which is born of the Spirit is spirit. Do not marvel that I said to you, 'You must be born again.' The wind blows where it wishes, and you hear the sound of it, but cannot tell where it comes from and where it goes. So is everyone who is born of the Spirit" (NKJV).

It's a bit of a mind bender, isn't it? By all appearances, nothing has changed, but that couldn't be further from the truth. Nicodemus struggled to understand it and I think many of us do too.

When we are born in the natural, we are born of the flesh. Our flesh is formed, and our soul comes alive in the womb with the help of our Creator, but our spirit man inside is not alive to God; we are only flesh... completely and solely carnal. Because of the sin of Adam and Eve, every person born physically is born dead in spirit and disconnected from true life found only in God.[6] Our family is merely our natural family related by natural blood. But, when we surrender to Christ, a miracle takes place on the inside, in the invisible spiritual realm, and our spirit-man is re-born coming alive to God and connected eternally to His heart and Spirit. We become part of God's family connected by the blood of Jesus shed on our behalf. Second Corinthians 5:17 tells us that we are new creations in Christ—not creations that have been renovated or spruced-up but brand-new creations. The old is completely done away with and the new is here!

> So from now on we don't look at anyone the way the world does. At one time we looked at Christ in that way. But we don't anymore. When anyone lives in Christ, the new creation has come. The old is gone! The new is here! All this is from God. He brought us back to himself through Christ's death on the cross. And he has given us the task of bringing others back to him through Christ (2 Cor. 5:16-18 NIRV).

Ephesians 2 also gives us great insight into how we have changed as children of God:

> ¹Once you were dead because of your disobedience and your many sins. ²You used to live in sin, just like the rest of the world, obeying the devil—the commander of the powers in the unseen world. He is the spirit at work in the hearts of those who refuse to obey God. ³All of us used to live that way, following the passionate desires and inclinations of our sinful nature. By our very nature we were subject to God's anger, just like everyone else. ⁴But God is so rich in mercy, and he loved us so much, ⁵that even though we were dead because of our sins, he gave us life when he raised Christ from the dead. (It is only by God's grace that you have been saved!) ⁶*For he raised us from the dead along with Christ and seated us with him in the heavenly realms* because we are united with Christ Jesus. ⁷So God can point to us in all future ages as examples of the incredible wealth of his grace and kindness toward us, as shown in all he has done for us who are united with Christ Jesus.... ¹⁰For we are God's masterpiece. He has created us anew in Christ Jesus, so we can do the good things he planned for us long ago (Ephesians 2:1-7; 10 NLT, emphasis added).

It never gets old reading about how God has transformed us spiritually! He has raised us up with Christ and seated us in heavenly places with Him. Jesus sits at the right-hand of God and this scripture passage is telling us that we sit there with Him. Our lives are hidden in Christ! We are His body. We are in heavenly places with Him—not physically of course, but spiritually speaking, we are. We are citizens of heaven (Philippians 3:20), Christ's ambassadors living on the earth re-presenting Him to the world (2 Cor. 5:20). And in Christ, we have become the righteousness of God (2 Cor. 5:21). We are a chosen generation, appointed, predestined to belong to Him, a royal priesthood, a holy nation, His own special people, bought at a price to belong to Him (1 Peter 2:9, 1 Cor. 6:20, Eph. 1:4-5).

The following is adapted from Neil T. Anderson's book, Victory Over the Darkness. In Christ, by His grace and mercy, we are:

- the salt of the earth (Matt. 5:13).
- the light of the world (Matt. 5:14).
- children of God (John 1:12).
- part of the true vine, a channel of Christ's life (John 15:1&5).
- Christ's friends (John 15:15).
- chosen and appointed by Christ to bear His fruit (John 15:16).
- slaves to righteousness (Romans 6:18).
- enslaved to God (Romans 6:22).
- sons and daughters of God; God is spiritually our Father (Romans 8:14-15; Galatians 3:26; 4:6).
- joint heirs with Christ, sharing in His inheritance with Him (Romans 8:17).
- temples of the Holy Spirit—dwelling places of God (1 Cor. 3:16; 6:19).
- united to the Lord and one spirit with Him (1 Cor. 6:17).
- members of Christ's body (1 Cor. 12:27; Eph. 5:30).

- reconciled to God and ministers of reconciliation (2 Cor. 5:18-19).
- heirs of God (Gal. 4:6-7).
- saints (1 Cor. 1:2; Eph. 1:1; Phil. 1:1; Col. 1:2).
- prisoners of Christ (Eph. 3:1; 4:1).
- righteous and holy (Eph. 4:24).
- hidden with Christ in God (Col. 3:3).
- expressions of the life of Christ because He is our life (Col. 3:4).
- chosen of God, holy and dearly loved (Col. 3:12; 1 Thess. 1:4).
- sons and daughters of light and not of darkness (1 Thess. 5:5).
- holy partakers of a heavenly calling (Heb. 3:1).
- partakers of Christ; we share in His life (Heb. 3:14).
- God's living stones being built up in Christ as a spiritual house (1 Peter 2:5).
- aliens and strangers to this world in which we temporarily live (1 Peter 2:11 AMP).
- children of God who will resemble Him when He returns (1 John 3:2).
- complete in Christ (Col. 2:10).
- overcomers (1 John 5:4, "For every child of God defeats this evil world, and we achieve this victory through our faith." NLT).
- safe from harm—the devil cannot touch us (1 John 5:18, "We know that God's children do not make a practice of sinning, for God's Son holds them securely, and the evil one cannot touch them." NLT).

Because we are now Christ's own possession, we also have access to His victory over the devil and according to Luke

10:19, He has given us authority in Him to overcome all the power of the devil. Luke 10:19 (NKJV) says:

> **BEHOLD, I GIVE YOU THE AUTHORITY TO TRAMPLE ON SERPENTS AND SCORPIONS, AND OVER ALL THE POWER OF THE ENEMY, AND NOTHING SHALL BY ANY MEANS HURT YOU.**

I pray that you are encouraged by that amazing list of truths about you... in Christ. None of it is true because of what you have done. We cannot take any credit or glory. Instead, it is ALL true purely because of Christ's sacrifice for us. It is all God's doing.

Here's the mystery in it all. We actually don't walk it out perfectly yet, do we? But we can still claim it as true RIGHT NOW, because God says it is true right now. God gives us *everything* up front (because of His amazing grace). He credits our identity as being pure and holy just like Jesus BEFORE we are able to walk it out perfectly because He knows He is able to transform us into the image of His Son as we submit to Him. And He is already executing that plan in you and in me!

I choose to believe God's Word about me *despite* my periodic failures. What about you? Will you choose to believe it for yourself? God's Word is truth. Let's stand on it for ourselves and resist anything contrary to it.

There is power in believing the truth about yourself and declaring it out loud. It empowers you and sets you up to behave like the favored son or daughter that you are.

Many Christians struggle with their behavior. They can't seem to get out of a pattern of sin. Sometimes deliverance is needed but sometimes it's simply a matter of renouncing the lies they've believed about their identity. If they believe that they are a no good looser, they will act like a no good looser. But if they renounce those self-deprecating thoughts and believe the truth instead, they will begin to behave like the son or daughter that they are.

At the end of Romans 7, Paul describes what we all feel at times: a tug of war happening within us between the flesh and spirit. We do what we don't want to do, and we don't do what we ought to do, and it can feel frustrating. Thankfully, Paul reminds us in Romans 8:1-2 as follows:

> There is therefore now no condemnation to those who are in Christ Jesus, who do not walk according to the flesh, but according to the Spirit. For the law of the Spirit of life in Christ Jesus has made me free from the law of sin and death (NKJV).

I find making the following declaration out loud over myself most helpful: "Because I am in Christ, I have been set free from the law of sin and death. It no longer has any more power over me. I am free to choose not to sin! I am free to choose holiness. I am free to do what is right."

Some Christians, after identifying with Christ in His death and resurrection, still believe they are "a sinner saved by grace." But this is not true! We've already been *spiritually* resurrected! This means we are saints. No longer sinners.

Yes, we've been saved by grace. And yes, sometimes the flesh that is supposed to be dead tries to rise up again, but "sinner" is no longer our identity. Identifying the lies that we believe about ourselves and replacing them with truth sets us free to live victoriously.

> It is for freedom that Christ has set us free. Stand firm, then, and do not let yourselves be burdened again by a yoke of slavery (to the law or a need to be perfect in your own strength) (Gal. 5:1a NIV, brackets added).

> You who are trying to be justified by the law have been alienated from Christ; you have fallen away from grace. For through the Spirit we eagerly await *by faith* the righteousness for which we hope (Gal. 5:4-5 NIV, emphasis added).

Praise the Lord.

Lastly, our struggle with the enemy is not a power struggle. We are on the same team with Jesus—God's team—so there is no contest. Satan doesn't have a chance. No...

> **OUR STRUGGLE AGAINST THE DEVIL IS NOT ABOUT POWER; IT'S ABOUT TRUTH AND OUR BOLDNESS AND WILLINGNESS TO STAND ON IT.**

And you shall know the truth, and the truth shall make you free (John 8:32 NKJV).

Rise up, daughter of God! Rise up, son of God! It's time to stop allowing the enemy to lie to you and push you around.

God is backing you up. Your Father is right behind you enforcing His victory through you.

SPIRITUAL PROTECTION

Several years ago, around Christmas time, when my children were young, I remember contemplating how challenging parenting was and how much responsibility it is. I mean... we're literally creating and forging new human beings! A good portion of a person's success in life is due to how they were parented, cared for, and brought up. Talk about pressure! Is there any other job with so much riding on just one or two people? Perhaps, but still! It's a lot.

As I contemplated my role as a mother and the shear craziness of God to entrust me with small humans, I thought of Jesus and how God trusted Mary, a young girl, maybe fourteen years old, with His Son. Wow. I asked God in my heart, *why wouldn't You choose someone a bit older? With a bit more life experience and wisdom?* And He quickly revealed to me that He doesn't give us our children expecting us to do *all* the work. He gives us our children with the full intention of co-parenting with us. He never leaves us alone in this tumultuous journey. When we miss it, He fills in the gaps. When our kids are off somewhere else, without us, He is there with them. He never leaves them—even when they haven't yet fully surrendered to Him, God is still with them and young children especially, easily discern His presence.

Just quickly, let me tell you a story from my own life. When I was only fourteen, I had my first boyfriend named Mark, and I had gone to the army barracks in town to meet him. He was in the cadets' program. My mom was supposed to pick me up at the gate at 10pm. So, Mark walked me there but left, assuming my mom would be there any minute. Unfortunately, she wasn't. I waited and waited. I walked to the main street and asked to use the telephone (this was before cell phones) at a corner store but was denied. I walked back to the gate at the barracks and waited again. It was dark and I was frightened. Even as I walked back through the park to the barracks, I could hear someone behind me. It was all I could do not to break out into a sprint. I prayed as I walked trying to remain calm.

As I continued to wait at the gate terrified, suddenly I saw across the small residential street, a large German Shepherd. I was a bit nervous of the dog at first as it was very large, but it didn't come any closer. He stayed where he was. He looked directly at me though, and I at him. Our eyes locked. After a few moments, he lied down and remained there until my mom finally showed up at about 11pm.

I knew without a doubt, as I sat staring at the dog and the dog staring back, that God had sent that dog to be with me—

to give me a sense of peace and protection. And as I sat, I thanked God for His protection and answering my prayer.

God is orchestrating all sorts of things behind the scenes of your children's lives, including swaying the hearts of your children toward His ways, helping them make good decisions, watching out for them and providing for their protection in various ways.

That day around Christmas when my children were young, I was very thankful for the revelation God gave me; it took the pressure off me as He promised to carry the load. I realized I didn't need to be the perfect parent because I had a perfect God helping me.

I think the best scripture to help us begin to think about the spiritual protection that the Lord provides for us and our family is Psalm 91. It is one that I have had to meditate on frequently, over the last number of years especially.

I am going to share Psalm 91 from The Passion Translation here as I sense that we need to hear it fresh again—with new ears. Reading a familiar passage of scripture in a different translation, helps us to hear it better and receive it again. So here goes. . . read it slowly and really hear what is being said to you in this moment:

> ¹*When you abide under the shadow of Shaddai*, you are hidden in the strength of God Most High. ²He's the hope that holds me and the stronghold to shelter me, the only God for me, and my great confidence. ³He will rescue you from every hidden trap of the enemy, and he will protect you from false accusation and any deadly curse. ⁴His massive arms are wrapped around you, protecting you. You can

run under his covering of majesty and hide. His arms of faithfulness are a shield keeping you from harm. ⁵You will never worry about an attack of demonic forces at night nor have to fear a spirit of darkness coming against you. ⁶Don't fear a thing! Whether by night or by day, demonic danger will not trouble you, nor will the powers of evil be launched against you. ⁷Even in a time of disaster, with thousands and thousands being killed, you will remain unscathed and unharmed. ⁸You will be a spectator as the wicked perish in judgment, for they will be paid back for what they have done! ⁹⁻¹⁰*When we live our lives within the shadow of God Most High*, our secret hiding place, we will always be shielded from harm. How then could evil prevail against us or disease infect us? ¹¹God sends angels with special orders to protect you wherever you go, defending you from all harm. ¹²If you walk into a trap, they'll be there for you and keep you from stumbling. ¹³You'll even walk unharmed among the fiercest powers of darkness, trampling every one of them beneath your feet! ¹⁴For here is what the Lord has spoken to me: "*Because you loved me, delighted in me, and have been loyal to my name*, I will greatly protect you. ¹⁵I will answer your cry for help every time you pray, and you will feel my presence in your time of trouble. I will deliver you and bring you honor. ¹⁶I will satisfy you with a full life and with all that I do for you. For you will enjoy the fullness of my salvation!" (Psalm 91 TPT, italics added).

Wow. That's so good! Isn't it?

This chapter of Psalm is packed full of amazing promises from God regarding His protection over us, but did you notice the parts I italicized? *"When you abide under the shadow of Shaddai..."* *"When we live our lives within the shadow of God Most High..."* *"Because you loved me, delighted in me, and have been loyal to my name..."* These are statements that identify *our* part in the promise. In fact, God's promises of protection are *contingent* on us doing these things. If we don't *abide with God* or *live our lives within the shadow of God...* if we don't *delight in Him*, if we're not *loyal to His name*, we could find ourselves in trouble. So, the key to experiencing the protection of the Lord is to be *faithful to Him*.

Think about what abiding with God is. *Abiding with* means *staying with, living with continually, not going in and out, but remaining*. And we abide with God when He is number one, when we honor Him well with our actions, words, and heart attitude, when we follow His ways and when we intentionally look for and discern His presence with us continually (even in moments of chaos and potential fear).

Doing church on Sunday mornings and then living your life on your own without Him through the week, however you want, is not abiding with Him. Abiding with Him is *recognizing and honoring His presence with you at all times*, reading His Word, and talking with Him every day, making Him the priority of your everyday life. When we do this, we live under His shadow, and His shadow becomes our protection. Much like an umbrella protects you from the rain, God's shadow protects us from harm and evil forces. Praise God!

Now, having said that, perhaps you're realizing you haven't been abiding perfectly. Well, I haven't either. The good news is the following: God knew we wouldn't, so He made a way for us to continue to experience His protection despite our weakness. We do this through repentance. Repentance activates God's mercy and grace on our behalf.

God sent His Son Jesus to atone for our sin and weaknesses so He could be in relationship with us again. He has given us grace. However, we should never think that we can take advantage of that grace. God cannot be mocked. The purpose of grace is not to give us an excuse not to make the effort. Instead...

> **GRACE EMPOWERS US TO DO WHAT GOD HAS CALLED US TO DO—TO ABIDE UNDER HIS SHADOW, TO LOVE HIM, DELIGHT IN HIM, AND TO BE LOYAL TO HIS NAME.**

So how do we repent? Well, first let me tell you that repentance is not feeling bad about yourself nor about what you have done. Repentance is not wallowing in your weaknesses. It may include a sense of grief and sorrow over your weakness, but a spirit of repentance does not hold us there. It is not a heaviness that sits on us nor is it worldly sorrow that causes us to remain in regret. A spirit of repentance *propels* us to *change our mind*, to recognize we have been going in the wrong direction and causes us to turn around. It causes us to stop, turn and head back to God where we belong.

Second Corinthians 7:10 says, "Godly sorrow brings repentance that leads to salvation and leaves no regret, but worldly sorrow brings death." We are not meant to be in sorrow without hope. There is always hope and there is ALWAYS opportunity to turn around and be *empowered by the Holy Spirit* to do better and to be victorious. Resist the lie that would want to convince you that God is *done* waiting for you to get it right. No! God is longsuffering and loves you despite how many times you need to repent and turn around. As long as your heart is set on honoring God and getting there with Him, there is no limit on how many times He will forgive you.

Now because I have heard from some that they don't know *how* to repent, let me help you. Share your heart with God. Make confession and ask for forgiveness. It may sound something like this:

> "Lord, I confess that I have not been abiding in You like I should. I have not made You, nor following Your ways my priority. I repent. Please forgive me. Thank You for Your forgiveness; I receive it in its fullness.[7] Help me Lord to make the adjustments in my life that will put You in Your proper place—on the throne of my heart. I ask You Holy Spirit to remind me that You are with me every morning and as I go about my day. Thank You for empowering me to put You first. In Jesus' name, amen."

Now, after you repent, it's time to put change into motion. To help you get into a spiritual rhythm with God, start by sticking a note on your bathroom mirror that says, *ABIDE*, to remind yourself. Perhaps write out some favourite Bible verses and post those where you will see them. This will get your mind thinking in the right direction each day. Perhaps Joshua 1:9 is a good one:

> Have I not commanded you? Be strong and of good courage; do not be afraid, nor be dismayed, for the LORD your God *is* with you wherever you go" (NKJV).

Every morning, consider reading a devotional and spending fifteen to twenty minutes in prayer and worship. Commit your day to God. For example, "Lord, I commit my day to You. Thank You for being with me. Help me to discern Your presence and leading throughout my activities, work, and commitments. Thank You for protecting me and my/our children. In Jesus' name, amen." Play worship music in your home and in your car as you drive.

Make use of other strategies to infuse faith, worship, and prayer into your day. Change the wallpaper on your phone to an image with a favorite scripture. Now, every time you look at your phone, you are reminded of the Lord and Who He is for you. Fill your social media feed with encouragement from your favorite ministers. Post scripture on the window in front of the sink where you wash dishes and think on them as you work. And every time you feel anxious or stressed, turn your heart toward God and feel Him breathing strength and patience into you.

Every night before bed, take stock of your day. How many times did you talk to God throughout your day? It doesn't have to be a long conversation with Him, maybe it was just an "I love You, God," or "Help me Jesus. Show me where You are." Ask yourself, "Did I go through the whole day in my own strength, or did I look to the Lord for help in some way?" We can be resourceful on our own and many of us have been taught to be strong and *suck it up* but very often this gets in the way of our true surrender and reliance on God. If we're honest, we need Him more than we're willing to admit. Thank the Lord for Who He is on your behalf and what He has done for you, every night.

Lastly, put aside a few hours every week to do a Bible study, either on your own, with a friend for accountability or with a small group. Have some close friends who you can talk about God and the Word with. Incorporate Bible reading into your life—if not daily, at least twice a week as a starting point. Put it on your calendar if you must.

Practice abiding every day and you will get better and better at it as you grow, develop new habits and disciplines, and rely on Him more. Most importantly, love the Lord your God with all your heart, with all your soul, with all your mind and with all your strength and love your neighbor as yourself (Mark 12:30-31) and in faith, expect Him to meet with you. It is vital that you engage more than just your mental capacity with God. You must engage your spirit. God is Spirit, and in order to feel His presence we need to connect by the Spirit, in the spiritual realm.

※

The second scripture passage that I think you will find helpful, regarding spiritual protection is Psalm 139:1-18. As you read it, read it slowly and purposefully. Ask the Holy Spirit to speak to you. Understand that although King David wrote this about himself, we could have all written it about ourselves too. It applies to all of us. Again, from The Passion Translation, it reads:

> ¹Lord, you know everything there is to know about me. ²You perceive every movement of my heart and soul, and you understand my every thought before it even enters my mind. ³⁻⁴You are so intimately aware of me, Lord. You read my heart like an open book and you know all the words I'm about to speak before I even start a sentence! You know every step I will take before my journey even begins. ⁵You've gone into my future to prepare the way, and in kindness you follow behind me to spare me from the harm of my past. You have laid your hand on me! ⁶This is just too wonderful, deep, and incomprehensible! Your understanding of me brings me wonder and strength. ⁷Where could I go from your Spirit? Where could I run and hide from your face? ⁸If I go up to heaven, you're there! If I go down to the realm of the dead, you're there too! ⁹If I fly with wings into the shining dawn, you're there! If I fly into the radiant sunset, you're there waiting! ¹⁰Wherever I go, your hand will guide me; your strength will empower me. ¹¹It's impossible to disappear from you or to ask the darkness to hide me, for your presence is everywhere, bringing light into my night. ¹²There is no such thing as darkness with you. The night, to you, is as bright as the day; there's no difference between the two. ¹³You formed my innermost being, shaping my delicate inside and my intricate outside, and wove them all together in my mother's womb. ¹⁴I thank you, God,

for making me so mysteriously complex! Everything you do is marvellously breathtaking. It simply amazes me to think about it! How thoroughly you know me, Lord! [15]You even formed every bone in my body when you created me in the secret place; carefully, skillfully you shaped me from nothing to something. [16]You saw who you created me to be before I became me! Before I'd ever seen the light of day, the number of days you planned for me were already recorded in your book. [17-18]Every single moment you are thinking of me! How precious and wonderful to consider that you cherish me constantly in your every thought! O God, your desires toward me are more than the grains of sand on every shore! When I awake each morning, you're still with me."

This is my most favorite passage of scripture. I love it. It has helped me to heal from some difficult situations in my past.

- As you read this passage, what stood out to you? If you don't know, go back and read it again. Use a highlighter to mark the important bits.

Now, what stood out to you? Why do you think it stood out to you? I would suggest talking to God about this and making some notes. Usually, a Word in the Bible stands out to us because it is something we need. God wants to speak to you and minister to your heart through what you're reading. So how does the portion that stood out to you, minister to you? Does it give you an increased sense of peace in your heart? Does it address a fear you may have? Or does it address something you might believe which is perhaps not truth? Does this passage cause you to think differently in some way?

Spend some time with God, meditating and chewing on what you're learning.

Yes, even though we have God's promises for protection, as we've already said, we don't always do our part well, and we likely spent some time living apart from God as a pre-believer, so at times we have been vulnerable to painful circumstances. But here's the beauty in it all, God will always redeem what we've lost. He will always heal and bring something good out of it all. According to Romans 8:28, "And we know that in all things God works for the good of those who love him, who have been called according to his purpose" (NIV).

I saw a little video or what we call a "reel" on Facebook yesterday that said it well, "If God has not redeemed a situation, then God is not done. There is no such thing as tragedy in my life because God will redeem everything." Our pain has GREAT purpose; it will be used by God to form our character, put empathy in our heart for others and it *will* be used to help someone else in the future.

To help you deepen your relationship with the Lord and *abide* with Him, here is a list of studies you might want to check out:

1. *Not a Fan* by Kyle Idleman
2. *Starved* by Amy Seifert
3. *Surrendered* or *The Armor of God* by Priscilla Shirer
4. *How Much More* by Lisa Harper
5. *The Quest* or *Believing God* by Beth Moore

The above can be purchased at lifeway.com, or rightnowmedia.org. I would also recommend anything by

Lisa or John Bevere which can be purchased on their site, messengerinternational.org.

Lastly, the most powerful element for our protection is always the blood of Jesus and I would encourage you to declare and plead the blood of Jesus over you, your family and your home often—each time you are praying for your family in fact.

Do you remember the Israelites in Egypt and how they escaped? God sent Moses to Egypt to deliver Israel, but God hardened Pharoah's heart for a time so that he would not let them go. This lasted through twelve plagues until the very last one that killed every first-born Egyptian son and livestock in one night. Pharoah's own son was killed, and he was finally compelled to let the Israelites go. But how did the Israelite families survive the plague with everyone still alive? They survived by the blood of a spotless lamb smeared on the posts and lintel of each family's doorway, dripping down, creating a blood-barrier to the angel of death.

> Then Moses called for all the elders of Israel and said to them, "Pick out and take lambs for yourselves according to your families, and kill the Passover *lamb*. And you shall take a bunch of hyssop, dip *it* in the blood that *is* in the basin, and strike the lintel and the two doorposts with the blood that *is* in the basin. And none of you shall go out of the door of his house until morning. For the LORD will pass through to strike the Egyptians; and when He sees the blood on the lintel and on the two doorposts, the LORD will pass over the door and not allow the destroyer to come into your houses to strike *you* (Exodus 12:21-23 NKJV).

Just as the blood of a spotless lamb saved the Israelites from God's judgement on the first Passover, God sent His Son, Jesus, to be our Passover lamb to save *us* from God's wrath and judgement. So, spiritually speaking, dip the hyssop branch in the blood of Jesus, friends, and in prayer, strike the lintel and doorposts of your home to create the same blood-barrier, keeping your home protected. The blood of Jesus still works today completely delivering us from all evil and keeping us locked into the safety of God's grace, love, and favor.

Okay, let's continue our journey and build on our foundational knowledge so we can stand against the schemes of the enemy and experience victory in Jesus. Onward and upward!

DELIVERANCE: WHAT IS IT?

Deliverance simply put is the silencing of and perhaps the eviction of demonic spirits from our mind, will, emotions or body that may be tormenting us in our thoughts, perhaps attached to us or in us because of deeply rooted patterns of sin that we have participated in, lies of the enemy that we have been believing, traumatic experiences, or iniquity passed on to us from our ancestors.[2] Manifestations of demons may happen in the physical body (as in the woman in the temple who was bent over) or may happen primarily in the mind which then can have a domino affect, touching other areas of who we are. In the case of the latter, we are speaking about *strongholds* of the mind (2 Cor. 10:4) which

---

[2]Iniquity is *not* the same as sin. Iniquity is the propensity or bent to sin a certain way that has been passed down from previous generations (see Ex. 20:5, Ex. 34:7, Num. 14:18, Deut. 5:9).

keep a person locked into a way of thinking that is wrong, skewed, exaggerated or twisted. A *stronghold* in the mind is a fortified neuropathway which is defended and maintained by demons. I am using the term deliverance to describe freedom from demons in every area of our being.

The first debate I'd like to address is whether a Christian can have a demon affecting them in their soul (mind, will & emotions) or lodged in their body. It's normal to want to immediately and aggressively say, "No!" while grasping for a Bible verse to justify it because in all honesty, NO ONE wants to go *there*. And certainly no one wants to be the one who has a demon, but a lot of people who struggle with demons behave, for the most part, normally. They're not presenting like the demoniac from the Gadarenes in Luke 8:26-33, ripping their clothes off and living in a graveyard. Instead, they're struggling internally with tormenting thoughts and impulses they are trying to suppress or they're struggling to break out of a pattern of behavior or thinking that is not in line with God's purposes or plan.[3]

We like to think that when we get "saved" *everything* about us is *automatically* and *spontaneously* made new, but unfortunately, it's not. *Everything* is not made new in that one moment. No one has ever experienced complete transformation in spirit, soul, *and* body when they make a decision for Christ. We still have our earthly body after we get saved, don't we? We still battle against sickness after we

---

[3] Remember what Jesus said to Peter in Matthew 16:23? "Get behind Me, Satan! You are an offense to Me, for you are not mindful of the things of God, but the things of men (NKJV). Even Peter was being deceived in his mind about the will of God (though at that time he did not have the Holy Spirit).

get saved, don't we? We still struggle with sin habits and various other things after we get saved, right? We still need to have our mind renewed—in a sense re-programed—according to the Word of God, right?

Do Christians need deliverance? The answer, "No," is the tidy answer, but it's not the right answer. The right answer is, "Yes," because when we surrender to Christ and are saved, we are fully and completely healed and made whole in *spirit* only. The rest of us takes time. The rest of us takes a "laying it all down" and a surrendering of heart, mind, will, emotions, and desires, usually one piece at a time. Our soul is a complex, deep place where things get packed away and forgotten about. There are things still there that we don't even realize we never let go.

When that traumatic thing happened to you when you were nine, you didn't really understand it; all you really knew was that you felt confused, rejected and scared and all those feelings that didn't get processed got packed away into a tiny little box and stuffed down into your soul. Year after year, more little boxes got stacked on top of one another and stored away and before you realized it, you accepted the lies you heard from the *spirit of rejection*. You came into agreement with the lie that you were a reject, and that you would *always* be rejected by those who were supposed to love you. Am I speaking to someone? This is only one scenario that invites a demon to attach to us. There are so many more.

Unfortunately, we tend to act like hoarders when it comes to our heart and our emotions. We don't give things up easily and we are experts at trying to ignore and avoid pain.

We are a three-part being made in the image of God. We are primarily a spirit. We have a soul which consists of our mind, will, and emotions. And we live in a temporary physical *tent* which is our body. Because of the fall of Adam and Eve, every person that is born, is born dead to God and must be re-born by the Spirit to enter back into relationship with God. We do this by genuinely repenting for our sin, believing on the Lord Jesus Christ and being baptized. This is our born-again, salvation experience.

At the time that we are born again, it is our spirit that is born again, not our soul or our body. Our spirit is instantly re-born and renewed as the Holy Spirit takes up residence within us—our spirit and the Holy Spirit together in union, in our inner most being. It's a beautiful thing! We are positionally sanctified before God the Father. He accepts us just as we are as we become the righteousness of Christ, spiritually.

At the same time as we are born again *in spirit*, the *process* of sanctification in our soul begins. Second Corinthians 3:18 says:

> But we all, with unveiled face, beholding as in a mirror the glory of the Lord, *are being transformed into the same image from glory to glory*, just as by the Spirit of the Lord (NKJV, italics added).

Romans 12:2 says:

> And do not be conformed to this world [any longer with its superficial values and customs], but be transformed *and* progressively changed [as you mature spiritually] by the renewing of your mind [focusing on godly values and ethical attitudes], so that you may prove [for yourselves] what the will of

God is, that which is good and acceptable and perfect [in His plan and purpose for you] (AMP).

The process of sanctification looks different for everyone, but it is a process of healing and refining that we lean into and invite the Holy Spirit to do. The speed of the process is very much determined by how we are willing to invite God in and allow the Holy Spirit to do what He wants to do. This process can also affect our body and cause it to manifest healing as our body will very often follow what happens in our mind, will, and emotions.[8] Part of this process is the deliverance from tormenting spirits that we have been talking about.

In the beginning, it was God's pleasure and desire to give us all free will so that we would love Him out of our own choice, not by some forced obligation. So, the human part of us, our soul, operates by free will; God has given us dominion over our own soul. We have the choice to submit to the Holy Spirit in our mind, will, and emotions and we have the choice not to. The Holy Spirit does not force Himself on us but waits for us to hand over to Him all we've held onto. We have a responsibility to partner with the Holy Spirit to bring about our own transformation by His power. Again, the verse from 1 Peter 5:8 begins, "Be sober, be vigilant..." and we know from elementary school that this type of statement called a "command" infers the pronoun "You" at the beginning. "(You) be sober, (You) be vigilant..." God is not going to do that part for you.

Sometimes a word picture or illustration helps us to understand difficult concepts. Let's consider the following illustration to help us understand how we can be oppressed by demons even though we're a Christian.

Imagine you lease a car. You don't own the car; it belongs to the car dealership, but it's on loan to you and you are responsible for its upkeep and maintenance. You drive the car anywhere you want and use it for whatever purpose your heart desires. You can also invite whomever you want, to ride along with you in the passenger seat.

Imagine also, that certain "less-desirable" passengers get to ride along with you *by default* based on the things that you do, participate in, carry forward from previous generations and don't let go of in your heart. These less-desirable passengers (demons) automatically get to ride with you, and they don't have to get out of the car until you stop giving them access, cut association with them and tell them to "get lost!"

You oversee that car on loan to you. You're responsible to take care of it. The owner of the car isn't responsible to put the right type of gas in the car; that's your job. The owner of the car isn't responsible to control who rides with you in the car. That's also your job! You are the one who opens and closes the door for your passengers according to your behavior and words. You have the freedom to choose who and what you fellowship with. If you entertain violence on a consistent basis, you open the door to your car to a spirit of violence which will ride with you for as long as you refuse to deal with your poor choices and command that thing to "Get out!"

Let's say you decide to believe on Jesus, and you become born-again. The Holy Spirit doesn't take over the whole car;

He becomes a new engine for your car and occupies whatever other space you invite Him into. The Holy Spirit gives your car an oil change and becomes your new turbo-powered engine, but the car is still *mostly* the same on the outside. Additionally, the passengers that are already in your car don't have to get out. They *only* get out when YOU stop giving them access (through your behaviors, words, and attitudes) and tell them to get out. The Holy Spirit doesn't cause them to leave because He is required to allow you to call the shots. He does not overpower your free will. He's a gentleman and isn't into controlling you or forcing anything on you.

Are you getting the parallel here? Our body and soul are on loan to us from God. He created them and gave them to us to manage properly. When we don't do that, we pay the consequences.

Now, I hope there's a witness in your spirit that what I'm saying is truth. However, I do know there might be some still not convinced. Unfortunately, there is no scripture that explicitly says that a Christian can or can not have a demon and we don't explicitly see anyone being delivered from demons after they've entered the church. (Although this does not necessarily mean it didn't happen, just that it wasn't recorded.) However, there is one place where I can see that it could have happened and that is with Simon the sorcerer in Acts 8:5-24.

In Acts eight, Philip went to preach in Samaria and the people were eager to hear what he had to say. The people responded favorably, and many believed and were baptized. Verse seven tells us that "many evil spirits were cast out, screaming as they left their victims" and many were healed from paralysis.

In that same town, there was a man named Simon who was a sorcerer, and he had amazed the local people with his magic. Verse thirteen tells us that even he believed Philip's message and was baptized. As a result, Simon began following Philip wherever he went. He was astonished by the signs and great miracles Philip performed. Let's look at verses 14-24 as follows:

> [14] When the apostles in Jerusalem heard that the people of Samaria had accepted God's message, they sent Peter and John there. [15] As soon as they arrived, they prayed for these new believers to receive the Holy Spirit. [16] The Holy Spirit had not yet come upon any of them, for they had only been baptized in the name of the Lord Jesus. [17] Then Peter and John laid their hands upon these believers, and they received the Holy Spirit. [18] When Simon [the sorcerer] saw that the Spirit was given when the apostles laid their hands on people, he offered them money to buy this power. [19] "Let me have this power, too," he exclaimed, "so that when I lay my hands on people, they will receive the Holy Spirit!" [20] But Peter replied, "May your money be destroyed with you for thinking God's gift can be bought! [21] You can have no part in this, for your heart is not right with God. [22] Repent of your wickedness and pray to the Lord. Perhaps he will forgive your evil thoughts, [23] for I can see that you are full of bitter jealousy and are held captive by sin." [24] "Pray to the Lord for me," Simon exclaimed, "that these terrible things you've said won't happen to me!" (Acts 8:14-24 NLT, brackets added)

Verse thirteen explicitly says, "Then Simon himself believed and was baptized..." so we can't say, "Oh well, maybe he didn't really believe." No, if this were the case, it would not have been recorded as such. So how is it that Simon was "full of bitter jealousy and held captive to sin" after having believed and been baptized? Well, Simon was used to being paid to perform magic and he was simply continuing in what he knew—what was familiar. Simon had been operating in demonic power and was held captive in his mind to that way of doing things. He needed deliverance! Simon needed deliverance from bitterness, jealousy, and the demonic powers he agreed with as he performed magic. Unfortunately, the Bible does not record what happened after Simon asked Peter to pray. I think that Peter would have prayed with him and helped him to get free through repentance and deliverance, but unfortunately, we don't know for sure because it is not recorded.

I also believe that a possible reason why we don't see people in the Bible being delivered after joining the church is that the Apostles operated in their evangelistic anointing differently than *most* do today. They operated in great power and discernment. Demons could not hide from them. Deliverance, was therefore, something that happened at the moment of decision or baptism.

In the book of Acts, the Apostles very successfully followed the lead of the Holy Spirit when they preached the Gospel and brought people into the fellowship. It wasn't our westernized *short-cut* version that preaches a message and leads someone in a *sinner's prayer*. No! Deliverance and baptism were part of the original blueprint of conversion. Before anyone came into the church, their sin was turned away from *and their demons were dealt with*. Everyone who was part of the church was expected to follow Christ's example of holiness, so they needed to be *cleaned up* and set free as much as possible to avoid getting tripped up or enticed back into sin.

The Apostles in the book of Acts did not simply preach Jesus and have people say a little prayer. The apostles in Acts preached in the power of the Holy Spirit, *immediately* baptized those who believed, in water *and* in the Holy Spirit, healed those who needed to be healed, and delivered those who needed to be delivered. They did not leave people demonized. In fact, they preached with such anointing and power that very often people were spontaneously delivered. We just saw this happening in Acts 8 when Philip preached in Samaria. Today, there are also pockets of evangelistic ministers doing this outside of the typical church. If you follow Kayla Gabbard on social media, you will see her baptizing people in the power of the Holy Spirit and *immediately* praying deliverance over them when they come out of the water. It's a beautiful thing. It doesn't happen in the local church because spontaneous baptism and deliverance isn't tidy and predictable. It can be messy, and it doesn't fit into the westernized church format.

This is the blueprint modeled by the apostles: make disciples by preaching, teaching, delivering, healing, and baptizing, all at the same outreach event. Unfortunately, very often we miss two out of five of these steps.

There are two "great commissions" given by Jesus that confirms the blueprint. One is found in Matthew 28:18-20 and one is found in Mark 16:15-18. Let's look at them.

Matthew says the following:

> And Jesus came and spoke to them, saying, "All authority has been given to Me in heaven and on earth. Go therefore and make disciples of all the nations, baptizing them in the name of the Father and of the Son and of the Holy Spirit, teaching them to observe all things that I have commanded you; and lo, I am with you always, even to the end of the age." Amen (Matt. 28:18-20 NKJV).

Mark says the following:

> And He said to them, "Go into all the world and preach the gospel to every creature. He who believes and is baptized will be saved; but he who does not believe will be condemned. And these signs will follow those who believe: In My name they will cast out demons; they will speak with new tongues; they will take up serpents; and if they drink anything deadly, it will by no means hurt them; they will lay hands on the sick, and they will recover" (Mark 16:15-18 NKJV).

The commission found in Matthew simply says to "make disciples," "baptize them," and "teach them." I would suggest, however, that the process of "making disciples" would include delivering them from demons. Afterall, how can people be true disciples, following the commands of Jesus, living in holiness, and evangelizing others, if they haven't been set free from the demons that hold them back?

The commission in Mark includes the signs that should follow those who believe, and they include the casting out of demons. The westernized church likes to focus on the commission found in Matthew as it allows them to avoid the whole subject of deliverance. Unfortunately, because a large portion of the westernized church lacks power and doesn't operate in deliverance nor the gift of discerning of spirits, we have scores of Christians in the church who are still suffering with tormenting demonic spirits. No one has come along side them in power and helped them to be free. When they decided to believe and be baptized, deliverance was missed. And it would be easy to do that! It's not always obvious when someone has a demon. They tend to hide it well, plus, many oppressed people with physical manifestations are diagnosed by modern medicine, which conceals a spiritual problem as physical.

Having said all that, it is important to point out that one does not have to be delivered from demons in order to be saved. We see this in Mark, "He who believes and is baptized will be saved (Mark 16:16a NKJV). Period. But in order to live for Christ in this world, experience peace, and be effective in our assignments and calling, we absolutely need to be delivered from demons. Deliverance is about our peace and effectiveness here and now on the earth. Because demons attach to the yet *unhealed* parts of our flesh, as soon as our body gives out and we cross over to be with Jesus forever, we become COMPLETELY healed and any demon that may still be hanging out with us has to leave to find another body/soul to occupy. The demon does NOT affect the location of our eternity.

WE CAN BE SAVED WITHOUT DELIVERANCE, BUT WE'RE NOT FREE ON EARTH WITHOUT IT.

For clarity, I would like to also explain that Christians are not *possessed* by demons. Possession is about ownership and that term does not rightly describe how demons affect us. We are owned by Christ; we have been bought at a very high price (1 Cor. 6:20).

The original Greek word translated as *possessed*, in many biblical references, is *daimonizomai*. Daimonizomai does not mean *possession*. It means *to be under the power of a demon*.[9] A more accurate translation would therefore be *demonized* or possibly *oppressed*. Oppression is defined as *prolonged cruel or unjust treatment or control* and *mental pressure or distress*[10] which to me makes more sense. As a result, I always refer to being under the influence of a demon as being *oppressed*, *demonized*, or to *have a demon*.

Here's what the late Derek Prince, theologian and Bible teacher, who was one of the most reputable ministers of deliverance in his day, says in his book, *They Shall Expel Demons*, referring to Mark 1:23 which says, "Now there was a man in their synagogue *with an unclean spirit*" (NKJV):

> "In verse 23, when the NKJV says *with an unclean spirit*, the Greek actually says *in an unclean spirit*. Perhaps the nearest English equivalent would be *under the influence of an unclean spirit*.
>
> It is noteworthy that the New International Version translates this phrase *possessed by an evil spirit*. This exemplifies how translations can mislead us regarding the activity of evil spirits (or demons). Nothing in the original Greek justifies the use of the word *possessed*, with its suggestion of ownership. This translation is an accommodation

to traditional religious terminology that obscures the meaning of the original text."[11]

In conclusion, "possessed" by an evil spirit is not an accurate translation. Sometimes going back to the original language clarifies the truth within the nuance of scripture.

Who is Deliverance For?

Deliverance is for anyone who will repent, turn to Jesus (make Him their Lord) and be baptized as the scriptures tell us to do. It is also for anyone who has already taken these steps in obedience, at anytime. It is not something that *needs* to be done immediately or within the first few months of being a believer. It's better that way but deliverance can be done anytime. Also, it may not be something that happens all in one shot. Very often, people are healed and delivered in stages; each time the Lord goes a little bit deeper into the heart. Deliverance also can accompany deep healing or what some might call inner-healing or emotional healing. This is the healing of emotional wounds and lies that we believe associated with the trauma we may have endured.

Deliverance is not for those who are not ready to surrender their lives to Christ, however, binding the demons of antichrist, unbelief and pride prior to sharing the good news may be helpful so the spiritual eyes and ears of the hearer are open to understand their need for Jesus and Who Jesus is. It is best to follow the lead of the Holy Spirit and the Apostles in the book of Acts. If deliverance is needed for a pre-believer, go after it and expect it to manifest only *after* you have shared the good news of the Gospel, and they have accepted it. Signs and wonders *follow* the preaching of the Word.

Jesus told us in Luke 11:24-26:

> "When an impure spirit comes out of a person, it goes through arid places seeking rest and does not find it. Then it says, 'I will return to the house I left.' When it arrives, it finds the house swept clean and put in order. Then it goes and takes seven other spirits more wicked than itself, and they go in and live there. And the final condition of that person is worse than the first" (NIV).

So, we learn from this that it is very important the person that is being delivered is subsequently filled by the Holy Spirit, so they are NOT *put in order* and left empty. When we surrender to Christ authentically, the Holy Spirit comes to live in us. When we are baptized in the Holy Spirit, we are completely filled and empowered by the Holy Spirit and His power. However, scripture also tells us to be *continually* filled with the Spirit.

Ephesians 5:18 says, "Do not get drunk on wine, which leads to debauchery. Instead, be filled with the Spirit" (NIV). The phrase *be filled* was translated from a Greek verb in the *present perfect* tense which according to Chuck Smith's commentary on Blueletterbible.org indicates a continual filling, not a one-time occurrence.[12] This is further understood when we consider that Jesus described the presence of the Spirit within, to the woman at the well in John 7:38, as *rivers of living water*. Rivers flow. They are not stagnant bodies of water like wells, but one that continually flows in and out requiring an inlet that does not cease supplying the water.

Never cast a demon out of yourself or someone else without *also* asking the Holy Spirit to come and fill you or them *completely*, after deliverance.

Next, let's look at the many ways we can inadvertently invite demons to attach to us and the many circumstances that demons take advantage of to influence our behavior, thinking, emotions, and even health. In addition, we'll look at some red flags that may indicate someone is oppressed by demons.

FAST TRACK TO TROUBLE

How do We Become Demonized?

It's a great question. And an important one so we can prevent demonic oppression before it happens.

Demonic oppression can be passed down to us from our ancestors through iniquity and can also happen anytime we agree with the kingdom of darkness or *choose* to partner with it, knowingly or unknowingly. We partner with the kingdom of darkness when we choose to be entertained by it, make a *habit* of sinful behavior or thinking patterns, or hold onto bad memories, trauma, hurt feelings, wounds, and negative heart attitudes.

Being entertained by or partnering with darkness can look like any of the following:

- Watching horror movies.

- Playing games, electronic or otherwise, that involve occult images and practices such as: Magic Eight Ball, Ouija Board, Dungeons and Dragons and many others.
- Watching violent movies or videos.
- Playing violent video games involving fighting and murder. It does not matter if the characters are made of Lego or if they look hideous. All violence can have an adverse effect on us.
- Watching pornographic videos and looking at pornographic pictures.
- Participating in occult practices such as manifesting, palm reading, reading Tarot cards, psychic readings, astrology, numerology, hypnosis, astral projection, clairvoyance, black or white magic, automatic writing, table lifting, séance, levitation, telepathy, divination, spirit guides, blood pacts, Voodoo, fetishism, reading and believing in horoscopes and Zodiac signs, and chasing ghosts (which are actually demons pretending to be people who are deceased).
- Watching shows or movies that involve any of the above occult activities.
- Participating in any practice that attempts to know the future apart from God's wisdom and knowledge.
- Participating in any practice that is *rooted* in any other religion or worships any god other than the One true God of Abraham, Isaac, and Jacob, Yahweh, such as Yoga and martial arts.
- Participating in witchcraft, Wicca, Qabalah, Spiritualism, Rosicrucianism, Theosophy, Anthroposophy, Hermetic Order of the Golden Dawn, New

Age, Masonic Lodge, Job's Daughters, The Orange Order, The Shriners, any fraternity or sorority.
- Participating in any false religion or cult.
- Participating in any practice or prayer that attempts to control the actions of another person.
- Participating in any alternative healing practice that is *rooted* in anything spiritual other than our One true God, Jehovah-Rapha such as: Hypnosis, Reiki, Energy healing, healing crystals, ancient Chinese medicine including dry needling, acupuncture, and chiropractic care. (There tends to be a lot of push back on chiropractic but I wanted to mention it so you can seek the Lord about it. Like everything else, we need to look at how it came to be and where it originated. Chiropractic began in 1895 with Daniel David Palmer who was a spiritist (someone who consults spirits/demons). Wikipedia says this: "As an active spiritist D. D. Palmer said he "received chiropractic from the other world" from a deceased medical physician named Dr. Jim Atkinson."[13] So D.D. Palmer got the idea of chiropractic from talking to a dead person, which in actuality would have been a demon.)
- Overusing or misusing traditional medicine. For example: narcotic pain medication, antidepressants and stimulants.
- Looking to any false god or mythical god for healing or help in any way.
- Holding anything too tightly with an unwillingness to release it to God.
- Loving anything or anyone the same or more than God. God will not share the throne of your heart; He wants it all.

- Holding onto anger past sunset. ("And "don't sin by letting anger control you." Don't let the sun go down while you are still angry, for anger gives a foothold to the devil" (Eph. 4:26 NLT).)
- Not forgiving those who have hurt you. Not forgiving yourself.
- Holding onto offense and bitterness.
- Habitually lying, cheating, cussing, and stealing.
- Hating anyone in your heart.
- Dishonoring your mother and/or father.
- Committing murder or having an abortion.
- Remaining in a state of jealousy.
- Committing sexual sin such as adultery, fornication, compulsive masturbation, any kind of sexual deviance including sodomy, oral sex, homosexuality, pedophilia, sadomasochism, bestiality, incest, fantasy, and voyeurism.
- Making ungodly oaths and vows to yourself that sound like, "I will never..." or "I will always..." Let your "yes" be "yes" and your "no," "no." Nothing more. (Matthew 5:34-37 & James 5:12[14]).
- Looking down on others and holding bitter judgements against them.
- Walking in the disappointment of unmet expectations persistently. Unwilling to let go of expectations of others.
- Walking in pride and entitlement consistently.
- Being connected to and taught by a church that is Pharisaical which emphasizes rules over love and grace, does not love God well through an intimate connection with Him, looks down on others, and doesn't allow the Holy Spirit to move.

- Persistently taking on responsibility that is not yours.
- Persistently agreeing with fear, anxiety and worry.
- Being overly emotionally attached to and dependant on anything or anyone other than God. Believing that you can't live without someone or something is a strong indicator.
- Remaining in false guilt and condemnation.
- Giving up your hope and putting it on a shelf. Persistently agreeing with hopelessness, and hope deferred. (Proverbs 13:12, "Hope deferred makes the heart sick, But when the desire comes, it is a tree of life" (NKJV).)
- Knowingly or unknowingly, speaking curses over yourself or others, especially if it's the same statement/confession over and over.
- Treating others unjustly without repentance and changing your ways.
- Purposely causing harm to others or animals.
- Breaking covenant through divorce.
- As a child, experiencing the break-up of family because of divorce which causes trauma.
- Experiencing abuse of any kind or abusing others.
- Disobedience to God without repentance.
- Rebellion against God without repentance.
- Believing the lies of the devil over the truth of God.
- Experiencing an acute, sudden, traumatic event such as a car accident or medical emergency without discerning the presence of God with you.

For those who may believe that practicing any of the occult activities listed above is okay, please read Deuteronomy 18:9-13.[15] I will also say that the occult, New Age, secret societies or clubs like Freemasonry, Job's Daughters, and

Shriners, cults and false religions are all part of Satan's kingdom. They are not of God. There are only two sources of spiritual power: God and Satan. If you're not looking SOLELY to the One true God, Yahweh, in your club or activity and not believing the *full counsel* of scripture as outlined in the *whole* Bible, it's not of God. Period. Mixture is not allowed.

God has said, "You shall have no other gods before Me" (Exodus 20:3 NKJV). Any of the activities listed above is participating with and looking to spiritual power apart from God. This is idolatry. Not to mention, dabbling in and playing with demonic power is very dangerous. It may seem innocent at first, but remember the Bible tells us that Satan comes as an angel of light (2 Cor. 11:14). The light that he comes with is deceptive. It will only last a short time until he knows he's got you hooked, then he begins to make your life a living hell. I have heard stories of women practicing Wicca that initially *seemed* harmless until they continued in it and began to be tormented by demons.

Also consider the warning that God gives the people of Jerusalem through the prophet Jeremiah. In Jeremiah 2:13 God says to the people, *you have committed two sins. You have abandoned (forsaken) me, the spring of living water and you have dug your own cisterns that cannot hold water.* In other words, you have chosen to ignore me and my provision; instead, you've relied on yourselves. But guess what, all your efforts are useless. In fact, your arrogance will only get you in trouble. Further down, Jeremiah 2:19 says:

> Your wickedness will punish you; your backsliding will rebuke you. Consider then and realize how evil and bitter it is for you when you forsake the LORD

your God and have no awe of me," declares the Lord, the LORD Almighty" (NIV).

Thank God that when we repent and turn from our sin, Jesus takes the penalty that should have fallen on us. Amen?

This side of the cross, let's not trample the precious blood of Jesus underfoot and make a mockery of Him by thinking we can use grace as an excuse to do whatever we want.

What Makes a Religion a Cult?

Merriam-Webster defines a cult as *a religion regarded as unorthodox or spurious.*[16] Spurious means *of falsified or erroneously attributed origin—forged, and of a deceitful nature or quality.*[17] In Kingdom of the Cults, Walter Martin agrees that a cult is any religious group which differs significantly from the norm of our culture, which to me is vague, but defines it with a little more clarity by writing the following:

> "...a cult might also be defined as a group of people gathered about a specific person or person's misinterpretation of the Bible. For example, Jehovah's Witnesses are, for the most part, followers of the interpretations of Charles T. Russell and J.F. Rutherford... Jehovah's Witnesses today still look to the Watchtower organization and its Governing Body to understand the Bible. In fact, Jehovah's Witnesses are taught that they cannot understand the Bible without the organization explaining it to them."[18]

In summary, we can identify cults by the following characteristics:

1. They gather around one particular person's interpretation of scripture which usually errs significantly from the truth of the Word and the Holy Spirit.
2. They dispute the true spiritual identity of Christ as divine—the only begotten Son of God, sent by the Father. As a result, they do not worship Jesus as God. They may like Jesus, follow His teachings, and respect Him, but they do not worship Him as divine. Remember what Jesus asked Simon Peter at Caesarea Philippi in Matthew 16:15, "But what about you?" he asked. "Who do you say I am" (NIV)? Then Simon Peter answered, "You are the Messiah, the Son of the living God" (v.16 NIV, notice the uppercase "S" on Son). Verse 17 follows, "Jesus replied, "Blessed are you, Simon son of Jonah, for this was not revealed to you by flesh and blood, but by my Father in heaven" (NIV). Simon got it right! As well, Jesus was not conceived like we are conceived. His mother was a virgin, so Jesus was conceived by the seed of God Himself, NOT the seed of a man.
3. Their leader or leaders have consistent bad fruit in their life due to a lack of character and true divine direction.
4. The leader or the members (or both) may claim to be sinless, which is a direct contradiction to scripture. (See Romans 3:23 & 1 John 1:8-10.)
5. They may not see the Bible as the infallible *Word of God* at all or in its entirety; they may want to *cherry-pick* the scriptures and only read the ones that back up their beliefs the best.

It's important to note that we are speaking of religious groups who teach and believe a different gospel from the *true* Gospel presented in scripture, that involves the distortion of *CORE*

Christian beliefs. Some Christians may have differing opinions on peripheral things and practices, like full-immersion baptism or sprinkling, and that's okay; these disagreements are not differences that set a group apart as a cult.

Second Peter 2:1-2 says:

> But there were also false prophets in Israel, just as there will be false teachers among you. They will cleverly teach destructive heresies and even deny the Master who bought them. In this way, they will bring sudden destruction on themselves. Many will follow their evil teaching and shameful immorality. And because of these teachers, the way of truth will be slandered. In their greed they will make up clever lies to get hold of your money. But God condemned them long ago, and their destruction will not be delayed" (NLT).

Some religions that are considered cults are the following: Jehovah's Witness, Scientology, Christian Science, Unity, Witness Lee, The Way International, The Unification Church, The Unitarian/Universalist Church, Church of Jesus Christ of Latter Day Saints, Church of the Living Word, the Worldwide Church of God, The Theosophical Society, The Bahá'í Faith, Children of God, Swedenborgians, Hare Krishna and more.

Signs of Oppression

Signs that you _may_ be oppressed by a demon are as follows:

- Persistent feeling of heaviness or depression
- Persistent confusion in your mind

- Feeling excessively tired all the time
- Having pain for which there is no explanation
- Persistent headaches or migraines
- Recurring physical issues like UTI's
- Disease in your body
- Fear and anxiety
- Feeling constantly frustrated, irritable, and agitated and not being able to snap out of it
- Having persistent thoughts of suspicion toward others that you can't or don't rebuke and overcome
- Having persistent and controlling thoughts in third person like, "You're stupid."
- Having persistent thoughts that tell you to do bad things which you can't or don't rebuke and overcome
- Consistently feeling pressure to do bad things
- Consistently compelled to hurt others
- Addiction
- Not being able to control yourself or your thoughts
- Constantly critical toward others
- Being persistently stubborn, defiant, disagreeable, contentious, and argumentative
- Persistent disturbing dreams and/or sexual dreams
- Persistent thoughts of doubt and unbelief toward God and faith that you can't overcome
- Not being able to pray, listen to a sermon or sit still in church
- Not wanting to worship God
- Self-righteousness, putting heavy burdens on others, not giving anyone grace, looking down on others
- Hard heart/cold heart/unfeeling
- Do not like affection/frigidity

- Habitual outbursts of rage
- Rebellious against God
- Lack of self-control
- Saying things like, "I hate you!" or "I hate God!" or "I wish I were dead!"
- Hating yourself
- Self-harm
- Gender dysphoria
- Sexual perversion
- Watching pornography
- Obsession with sex; never satisfied
- Habitually rejecting others
- Not knowing how to love/not expressing love to others
- Persistent self-focus
- Lack of desire to serve in church or help others
- Hurting animals
- Obsession with violent games or videos
- Not being able to forget about a traumatic event/keep thinking about it and rehashing it in your mind
- Fear of fire
- Obsession with fire
- Fear of water
- Fear of anything that you cannot overcome or push yourself through
- Persistent tormenting thoughts of doom that control your mood
- Persistent accusing thoughts that you can't overcome
- Panic attacks
- You can't say "no" even though you want to
- Recurring miscarriage

- Barrenness

This list is not exhaustive, but I think you get the picture.

Let's move on and begin to prepare ourselves to win the battle for our kids.

Preparing Yourself to Stand

PREPARING YOUR SPIRIT

I baptize you with water for repentance, but he who is coming after me is mightier than I, whose sandals I am not worthy to carry. He will baptize you with the Holy Spirit and fire (Matthew 3:11 ESV).

Before we embark on this journey, we want to make sure it goes as smooth as possible, so we need to prepare our spirits. James 4:7 tell us to first submit to God, then resist the devil and he will flee. James 4:8-10 says:

> Come near to God and he will come near to you. Wash your hands, you sinners, and purify your hearts, you double-minded. Grieve, mourn and wail. Change your laughter to mourning and your joy to gloom. Humble yourselves before the Lord, and he will lift you up (NIV).

In these verses, James is basically describing what happens to someone when they sincerely become aware of their need for forgiveness and their need for Jesus and they surrender to Him.

For several years, I have been concerned that some in the church think they are born-again when they really aren't. Why? Because many have learned that all they need to do is say a little prayer—what they call the "sinner's prayer;" very often a leader will lead someone to repeat after him/her. All that happens is they recite something like, "Jesus, I believe You died for me and rose again. I invite You into my heart. Please be my Savior. Amen." Sometimes there isn't even any mention of repentance or turning away from sin. And I feel like there's this ambiguity as to whether people first, mean what they are praying, second, are really convicted of their need for forgiveness, third, have a true revelation of what Jesus did for them, and fourth, have surrendered their life to Christ. Do they even understand that complete *surrender* to Christ is the requirement?

We really don't want to attempt any of the prayers in this book without first knowing, without a doubt, that we are truly born-again, we are wearing the armor of God, and we are empowered through the baptism of the Holy Spirit.

I'm going to quote the following from my previous book entitled, *Position Yourself for Healing: Finding the Sweet Spot Where Healing Becomes Reality* just because it fits so nicely here:

"A true salvation experience begins with a revelation of one's need, a revelation of one's own sin and brokenness. It continues with a revelation from the Holy Spirit, of Jesus and His sacrifice for us personally, then a revelation of the goodness and kindness of God which then causes a person to fall in love with Jesus and on their knees in repentance. A true salvation experience is a change of heart and mind causing someone to stop and turn around, changing direction. It causes a person who is unknowingly headed for a cliff, to adjust their course so they turn around and head back to the arms of God. And it's this call back to God, back to love, that instigates and perpetuates a change in desires, through the Spirit, which leads to a change in behavior."[19]

Perhaps you're not an emotional person and that is fine; there may not be tears. But there does need to be a heart shift, and you are the only one who knows whether *that* really happened for you. Some people have only given their mental assent to the Gospel and I'm sorry to say, it's not enough. There must be a heart change too.

People who are truly born-again are certain and they "know that they know," they are changed by the power of God. Here's a great question: Is there any fruit that is consistent with repentance in your life? How have you changed?

Here's a few more questions: Are you currently living in sin somehow? If you do sin, are you grieved about it? Does it bother you?

Those who are truly born-again sense the conviction of the Holy Spirit each time they get off track and they make every effort with the help of the Holy Spirit to make it right. We're not perfect but by the grace of God we lean into His empowering and healing to get there.

If you are living with your partner and you're not married yet, either get married or live separately. Fornication is a sin before God, and you will get yourself in deep "you know what" by continuing to do what you're doing. STOP reading this book and deal with your sin first. You cannot attempt to come against demons for your family if you are agreeing with them in the bedroom or anywhere else. You will get yourself in trouble attempting to do this.

Next, let's talk about the baptism of the Holy Spirit. What does it mean to be baptized in the Holy Spirit? It means to be fully immersed in Him and saturated by Him, body, soul and spirit; just like your body is fully immersed and saturated with water when water baptized, the same is true of the Spirit except He also reaches your inner being. The baptism of the Holy Spirit is a separate experience from the salvation experience. Just like the disciples received the Holy Spirit two separate ways, so do we.

The first time the disciples received the Holy Spirit was in John 20:19-22. It happened after Jesus' resurrection, when Jesus appeared to the disciples showing them his pierced hands and side. He commissioned them and breathed on them saying, "Receive the Holy Spirit." Jesus breathed on them with the intent of imparting the Holy Spirit to them internally. As Jesus breathed out, they breathed in what Jesus released—the Holy Spirit. This impartation represents what happens for believers at the moment of salvation. It is the awakening of our spirit with new life and when the Holy Spirit joins with our spirit.

The second time the Holy Spirit was imparted to the disciples was in Acts 2, on the day of Pentecost. In Acts 1:5, Jesus gave the disciples instructions to remain in Jerusalem and wait for the "gift" His Father promised: "For John baptized with water, but in a few days you will be baptized with the Holy Spirit" (Acts 1:5 NIV). The apostles waited in Jerusalem as they were told and in due time, the Holy Spirit came spontaneously just as Jesus said He would:

> Suddenly a sound like the blowing of a violent wind came from heaven and filled the whole house where they were sitting. They saw what seemed to be tongues of fire that separated and came to rest on each of them. All of them were filled with the Holy Spirit and began to speak in other tongues as the Spirit enabled them (Acts 2:2-4 NIV).

The baptism in the Holy Spirit can happen spontaneously as you believe, surrender, open your heart to Him, and ask Jesus to baptize you in the Holy Spirit. It can happen as you read these words right here or as an anointed leader imparts the Spirit to you through the laying on of hands or as you listen to the Word being preached at church, in your car, or even at home.

We see Jesus being baptized in the Holy Spirit right after His water baptism in Matthew 3:16, "After his baptism, as Jesus came up out of the water, the heavens were opened, and he saw the Spirit of God descending like a dove and settling on him" (NLT). We see new believers being baptized in the Holy Spirit spontaneously as they listen to Peter share the Gospel in Acts 10:44 and we see others being baptized in the Holy Spirit with the laying on of hands in Acts 8:17 and Acts 19:6.

So why am I bringing this up in this book? Because it is the baptism of the Holy Spirit that will give you power. In Acts 1:1-8 Jesus tells His disciples to wait in Jerusalem for the Holy Spirit to come because the disciples were about to begin their ministry. In order for the disciples to do what they were called to do, Jesus knew they were going to need divine power. In Acts 1:8 Jesus says, "But *you will receive power* when the Holy Spirit comes on you; and you will be my witnesses in Jerusalem, and in all Judea and Samaria, and to the ends of the earth" (NIV emphasis added). The disciples could not be the witnesses they were called to be without the baptism of the Holy Spirit, and we can not be the parents and the prayer warriors we need to be on behalf of our children without the same. We need to be empowered!

If you have never been baptized in the Holy Spirit, please pray right now and ask Jesus to do this for you.

If you haven't asked for more of the Holy Spirit in a while, please ask right now and continue to ask going forward. We all need to be replenished with His power as we pour out to others.

Lastly, let's put on the armor of God.

Here is Ephesians 6:13-18:

> Therefore put on the full armor of God, so that when the day of evil comes, you may be able to stand your ground, and after you have done everything, to stand. Stand firm then, with the belt of truth buckled around your waist, with the breastplate of righteousness in place, and with your feet fitted with the readiness that comes from the gospel of peace. In addition to all this, take up the shield of faith, with which you can extinguish all the flaming arrows of the evil one. Take the helmet of salvation and the sword of the Spirit, which is the word of God. And pray in the Spirit on all

occasions with all kinds of prayers and requests. With this in mind, be alert and always keep on praying for all the Lord's people. (NIV)

I won't go into great detail but give a brief overview of each piece mentioned so we know what they are and how to wear them. Each piece protects us and helps us stand in victory.

The very first piece of armor Paul mentions is the very first piece a soldier would put on before going into battle. This is the belt, and it represents truth. This belt is not like the belts we think of today. It's not to tighten the waist of a pair of jeans nor is its purpose for style. Rather, Paul was referring to a wide supportive brace of sorts, like a girdle (shapewear) worn around a person's midsection or core. It was a vital piece of a soldier's armor as it gave the soldier support and helped him to carry the weight of the other pieces of armor like the breastplate. It also would have carried the soldier's sword and other weapons, like a tool belt.

When we wear truth like a supportive brace around our core, it helps us to stand under the weight of life and our responsibilities. And it helps us to discern what's right and wrong and even to discern the difference between what's right and what's *almost* right.

The questions are: What truth? Whose truth? And, How do we wear it? First, Paul is talking about the absolute truth of God's Word. In this confused world many people want to have their own version of what is true but there is only ONE absolute truth. Standing through the battle of life looks like aligning our thoughts, perspectives, opinions, and behaviors with the Word of God and discerning all things through it. Secondly, we wear the belt of truth by *believing* truth, *speaking* truth, *living* truth and allowing the Word of truth to read us—to tell us and show us where we are out of alignment with God.

So very often, we do Bible studies and take in information. We learn the stories and read about the miracles Jesus did, but we don't realize that there are spiritual principles in the text that the Lord wants us to apply to our own lives. He wants us to allow His Word and His precepts to shape our lives.

Next, the breastplate of righteousness protects our core, our heart, and our vital organs. The good news is righteousness is simply attributed to us through faith, but our faith must be proven by what we do. Here's James 2:21-24:

> Was not our father Abraham considered righteous for what he did when he offered his son Isaac on the altar? You see that his faith and his actions were working together, and his faith was made complete by what he did. And the scripture was fulfilled that says, "Abraham believed God, and it was credited to him as righteousness," and he was called God's friend. You see that a person is considered righteous by what they do and not by faith alone (NIV).

If we continue to sin after being born-again without repentance and turning away from it continually, we are not actively living in faith; we are undermining our faith, and righteousness therefore is hindered in our lives. We cannot claim to be righteous before God unless we are living holy in the empowerment of the Holy Spirit—not necessarily perfectly, but we are pressing into Jesus to get there and living a life of repentance. We are keeping short accounts with God, every day seeking the Holy Spirit to convict us of what we need to turn away from.

Next in the armor, we have the shoes of the Gospel of peace. These shoes protect our feet and make our feet ready and equipped to go anywhere God calls us, with boldness and sure footedness, as the sole of these shoes grip difficult terrain when needed. When we are diligent to remain in peace, not allowing anxiety or fear to creep in, we are protected and because Paul compares peace to shoes, we can know that the peace of God protects and guides our steps as well. It makes me think of Philippians 4:6-7:

> Do not be anxious about anything, but in every situation, by prayer and petition, with thanksgiving, present your requests to God. And the peace of God, which transcends all understanding, will guard your hearts and your minds in Christ Jesus (NIV).

And Proverbs 16:9:

> The mind of a person plans his way, But the Lord directs his steps (NASB).

According to Priscilla Shirer in the Armor of God study, these first three pieces of armor comprise our *daily uniform*[20]—what we need to wear every day, all day; truth, righteousness and peace equip us to run our race. The last three pieces of armor are ones that you "take up" when the battle gets heated—when you need to take care of business. These are the shield of faith, the helmet of salvation, and the sword of the Spirit.

The helmet of salvation protects our mind as we fight with the Word of God, and it provides freedom for us from destructive thought patterns. Salvation is not just about redemption and getting a ticket to heaven, but it also saves us from tormenting spirits of the mind in the here and now. Salvation changes the way we think and orients our thought patterns to God's, His ways and His truth. Salvation changes our spiritual DNA. It causes us to be re-born of the Spirit, as a new creation (2 Cor. 5:17), saved and set apart for Christ and holiness. Salvation sets us free completely and gives us hope for what is to come in eternity with Jesus. It is the *fullness* and *completeness* of salvation that, when *believed* and *personally claimed,* when we say with conviction, "This is mine!" fortifies our mind for Jesus.

What are the benefits of salvation? I'm glad you asked! Let's look at Psalm 103:1-5 to see a few:

> Bless the LORD, O my soul; And all that is within me, *bless* His holy name! Bless the LORD, O my soul, And forget not all His benefits: Who forgives all your iniquities, Who heals all your diseases, Who redeems your life from destruction, Who crowns you with lovingkindness and tender mercies, Who satisfies your mouth with *good things,* So *that* your youth is renewed like the eagle's (NKJV).

The shield of faith stops the fiery darts of the enemy sent to accuse and deceive us. And the sword of the Spirit is the Word of God that we need to know and declare out loud to counter any lie the enemy may throw at us.

The last piece of armor or weapon of warfare is praying in the Spirit. Praying in the Spirit means praying according to the Spirit and what He would want us to pray instead of praying what we think we should pray. So, connect with the Spirit, ask Him to lead you in prayer and trust that He does.

Praying in the Sprit also means praying in tongues. And we should do that often because it accomplishes so much more than we realize. It is a powerful weapon.

Finally, as a summary, these attributes are your armor and your weapons in the spirit realm: truth, righteousness, peace, faith, salvation, the Word of God, and prayer.

Preparing your spirit by confirming your salvation, turning away from sin, being baptized in the Holy Spirit, and wearing the armor of God will set you up for success in the upcoming chapters. Let's go and set our family free.

PREPARING YOUR HEART

Those who sow with tears will reap with songs of joy (Ps.126:5 NIV).

Good morning, daughter or son of God. I declare it is a good, good, *morning* for you no matter what time it actually is as you read these words, because it is the beginning of a *new day* for you. I know it may not *feel* like it yet, but a new day *is* dawning over you right now and new things are about to be revealed to you by the Spirit of God. The reading of this book, right here, marks the turning point in your parenting challenge when it goes from feeling exhausting and almost impossible to empowering and infused with strength and joy by the power of the Holy Ghost.

Sound too spiritual for you. That's okay. Hang in there my friend and just go with it for now. Take a risk. Step out onto the water for a moment and see what God will do for you. You're not going to sink. I PROMISE!

Let's begin with Psalm 30 from The Passion Translation as a declaration *in faith*. Remember that as followers of Christ we are exhorted to walk by faith and not by sight (2 Cor. 5:7), which means we expect breakthrough, healing, restoration, and victory over our enemies to come swiftly, so much so that we declare it to be our reality *before* we see it with our natural eyes. That is called faith. Faith is the *substance* of things hoped for and the *evidence* of things not *yet* seen (Hebrews 11:1). So here we go. Read it out loud:

> Lord, I will exalt you and lift you high, for you have lifted me up on high! Over all my boasting, gloating enemies, you made me to triumph. O Lord, my healing God, I cried out for a miracle and you healed me! You brought me back from the brink of death, from the depths below. Now here I am, alive and well, fully restored! O sing and make melody, you steadfast lovers of God. Give thanks to him every time you reflect on his holiness! I've learned that his anger lasts for a moment, but his loving favor lasts a lifetime! We may weep through the night, but at daybreak it will turn into shouts of ecstatic joy. (Psalm 30:1-5 TPT).

Perhaps the New International Version sounds more familiar to you. Here's verse five: "... weeping may stay for a night, but rejoicing comes in the morning." Rejoicing is coming. Joy *is* coming! It may still *feel* heavy, but you can believe that joy is coming because it's true. Believe it with all your heart, for our God is a consuming fire and He is dealing with your enemies as we speak. And even as you have wept with heartache and weariness, you have continued to sow seeds of care, nurture, and love into the littles the Lord has given you, to the best of your ability, and God honors that. He honors your effort, and He honors your *yes* to Him, to your family, and to the responsibilities before you.

You don't have to be perfect. The Lord is not expecting perfection from you. He knows that you are dust, and He knows your limitations (Ps. 103:14). He covers you with His mercy and grace and beckons you to come—come and receive what only He can give you. Come and receive freedom from the weight of the world that has tried to crush you, from the guilt and the heaviness of heart. Come and receive refreshing from the Spring of Life that renews your hope and causes the dry and thirsty seedlings in your heart to raise their heads again and reach for the sun. The garden of God's Word in your heart is about to thrive once again. The life and zeal for Jesus and your family you once had is awakening again and coming back to full life.

What you just read is called a prophetic utterance from the Lord. It is a gift of the Holy Spirit that can operate through someone who is first submitted to the Lord Jesus and baptized in the Holy Spirit with His empowering presence.[21] The purpose of a prophetic utterance is for the encouragement and edification of the hearer or in this case, the reader.[22] It is a *now* word given in season to touch and bless others that communicates the heart of God for them. We know it is authentic when it touches our heart, lines up with the Word of God (the Bible) and God's character and carries an anointing from the Spirit.

Let's begin to prepare the soil of our heart.

Do you like to garden? Perhaps you used to enjoy gardening but now you don't have much time for it. I hear you. Regardless, you probably know that there is no point in sowing seeds or planting a seedling until you have prepared the ground to receive it. The ground may be hard and void of nutrients that a seed or plant will need to take root and grow well. And there's no point in planting anything in hard dry ground. It will be fruitless.

Jesus tells a parable about this in Matthew 13:3-9:

> Behold, a sower went out to sow. And as he sowed, some *seed* fell by the wayside; and the birds came and devoured them. Some fell on stony places, where they did not have much earth; and they immediately sprang up because they had no depth of earth. But when the sun was up they were scorched, and because they had no root they withered away. And some fell among thorns, and the thorns sprang up and choked them. But others fell on good ground and yielded a crop: some a hundredfold, some sixty, some thirty. He who has ears to hear, let him hear! (NKJV)

From this parable, we learn of four different places where seeds can be sown. First, the wayside or path, which is a place where the earth is downtrodden, where there is no loose soil, no place of incubation or nutrition, no opportunity for life at all—where the birds just come and eat up the seeds.

Secondly, there are stony places where there are a lot of stones amongst the soil and under the soil—where the soil doesn't have depth for the roots to go down deep. These seeds open and sprout but the sun scorches them, and they end up withering and dying. No fruit is yielded.

Third, seeds can be sown in soil among thorns, but the thorns end up choking the seedlings and killing them. Again, no fruit is yielded.

Fourth and last, seeds can be sown in good soil—soil that has depth, that has been cleared of thorns and has been cultivated, turned, broken up, watered and infused with fertilizer. Good soil is the only soil that is worth sowing into. Good soil that has been prepared and cultivated to bring forth a harvest, this is where our efforts pay off. Yes, the garden needs to be tended to as well, even after the seeds are planted, but preparation or lack there of is what makes or breaks any kind of harvest.

Why are we talking about this? Well, I'm sowing seeds as I write and there's much more to come. I don't want to waste anyone's time. There really is no point in me writing or you reading unless your heart is prepared to receive what is sown.

So, when Jesus explains the parable of the sower to His disciples in Mattew 13:19-23, He explains that the seeds that fall upon the path are seeds that are falling upon hearts that *completely* lack understanding. If you've read this far, I know you're a Christ follower, so I don't think this scenario applies to us now.

The seeds that fall in the soil that lacks depth because of stones, describe someone who has struggled to allow the roots of the truth of God's Word and His Kingdom to go deep into their heart. The *stones* that prevent this deep rooting could represent hardness or coldness of heart. The *thorns* that choke the Word out of someone's heart represent the worries of this life and the deceitfulness of wealth (verse 22). I would suggest that the *worries* of this life could result, among other things, from the *wounds* inflicted on us in our past.

So, as we begin this journey together, the Lord is asking for your permission to do a little cultivation in your heart. Would you be willing to allow Him access? Hopefully your answer is "yes." Even "maybe" will do for now. Perhaps you want to know exactly what He means by *cultivation* first and I completely understand if you do. Keep reading my friend.

Every couple, as they begin to start a family inevitably contemplate their upcoming parenting journey with excitement and anticipation, and I think usually there is a bit of fear too mixed in there—fear of the unknown and fear of not doing it well. (I think a little bit of fear in this area is healthy as we know children are a huge responsibility.) The same couples also have likely formed opinions, possibly very strong opinions about their own parents' parenting style based on how their own heart has survived or been affected by it. I think it's only normal to begin to form our own parenting style based on what we feel our parents did right or did horribly wrong. There is a danger in this, however, if we allow our heart to digress into lasting anger and bitter judgements against our parents.

I can speak from experience. For many years I was *angry* and *bitter* toward my mom for various legitimate reasons and carried emotional scars from paternal abuse. The *hate* I held in my heart and the *judgements* against my mom and dad prevented me from even becoming pregnant when we first started trying. It wasn't until God put His finger on these things that my destructive attitudes were brought into the light, confessed, surrendered, and healed and I eventually was able to birth our own biological children. My entire story can be read in my first book, *Barren No More*, available on Amazon, which details my emotional journey from barrenness to successfully birthing our four children.

In various places in scripture, we are commanded to honor our mother and father, *so that* our days would be long, and it would go well for us (Ex. 20:12, Deut. 5:16). Ephesians 4:26-27 warns us against anger, "In your anger do not sin': Do not let the sun go down while you are still angry, and do not give the devil a foothold" (NIV). We are told in Hebrews 12:14-15:

> Make every effort to live in peace with everyone and to be holy; without holiness no one will see the Lord. See to it that no one falls short of the grace of God and that no bitter root grows up to cause trouble and defile many (NIV).

First John 3:15 says, "Anyone who hates a brother or sister is a murderer, and you know that no murderer has eternal life residing in him" (NIV). Matthew 6:14-15 says, "For if you forgive other people when they sin against you, your heavenly Father will also forgive you. But if you do not forgive others their sins, your Father will not forgive your sins" (NIV). And finally, we are warned against judging others in Matthew 7:1-2, "Do not judge, or you too will be judged. For in the same way you judge others, you will be judged, and with the measure you use, it will be measured to you" (NIV).

So, all these things: dishonor toward our mother and father, anger held onto past sundown, bitterness, hate, unforgiveness, and judging others (looking down on them) ALL put us in an extremely vulnerable position to be harassed by the enemy and to experience adversity, strife, chaos, and all kinds of problems beyond our ability to handle. That's the bad news.

I know, yes, many have been through a very tough childhood with severely authoritarian parents (especially those who grew up in the church), including me. Many have not had close, loving relationship with their parents, and they know that the way they were parented should not be repeated. That's good. It's good to know that. But we can know that without being hateful and/or looking down on our parents and judging them with bitterness. I pray you hear what I'm saying.

Parents, for the most part, do the best they can with what they know at the time. And we must remember that our parents also had a childhood; we don't know what they endured and how they were hurt by their own parents. If they did not forgive their parents, the wounds that they accumulated in childhood would have caused them to act in less than loving and godly ways toward us. It's a chain of pain that doesn't stop until someone decides to forgive and surrender their right to be angry and offended to Jesus.

I am 99.9% sure my mother was abused in many ways by her father, including sexually, and she never healed from that until she crossed over into glory with Jesus. Think about how that would have affected how she acted and parented. She was full of fear—full of anxiety about the future and couldn't stop making the protection of herself her number one priority. How does a parent make their child feel safe and protected when the parent themself is not secure in their own safety? They can't. A sense of neglect and a lack of love in the child's heart is inevitable.

You know from your own parenting that *good* parenting is about self-sacrifice and putting the needs of others first. Although at times we *do* need to make self-care a priority, so we continue to feel human (like when you haven't showered in a week!), children need A LOT of care—physically, mentally, emotionally and spiritually. And *all that* takes a lot of time and energy. If a parent is captured or tormented in their own mind by insecurity, fear, worry, and anxiety, their children will suffer.

Before we get to the good news (we will get there!), one last thing that makes us vulnerable to the enemy is when we make promises to ourselves that sound something like: "I'm NEVER going to treat my kids the way I was treated," or "I'm NEVER going to act like my parents did," or "I'm NEVER going to do that to my kids," or "I'm going to love my kids properly," or "I'm going to treat my kids fairly," or "I'm ALWAYS going to listen to my kids." Does any of this sound familiar? Has any of it come out or your mouth or heart? All these statements and anything that sounds similar are called, *vows to self*. They are promises that you make to yourself that are rooted in bitter judgement against your parents. The hard truth is, you would not be making these promises if you were not *already* bitter about your parents' fallen parenting ability.

When it comes to the promises you make to yourself, the bitter judgement is only the first issue; there is a second. We make promises like this because we (don't shoot the messenger), deep down, think we are better than them— better at making decisions, better at keeping our cool, and smarter at parenting. Sorry my friend, I know it hurts. But we *must* keep it real. This is the only way we're going to get free.

Unfortunately, the spirit that causes us to make promises to ourselves out of bitter judgement is called pride, arrogance and haughtiness. It comes from an elevated sense of self-importance and ability. It's good to be confident but your confidence needs to be rooted in God. I like to call it Godfidence. We ALL need to stay humble and realize that we need God to help us on our parenting journeys. Not one of us can do it well without Him! I invite you now to agree with God about your need to repent for pride.

Matthew 5:33-37 gives us good direction when it comes to oaths, vows or promises to self:

> Again, you have heard that it was said to the people long ago, 'Do not break your oath, but fulfill to the Lord the vows you have made.' But I tell you, do not swear an oath at all: either by heaven, for it is God's throne; or by the earth, for it is his footstool; or by Jerusalem, for it is the city of the Great King. And do not swear by your head, for you cannot make even one hair white or black. All you need to say is simply 'Yes' or 'No'; anything beyond this comes from the evil one (NIV).

Okay, so this is the good news . . . there is a way out of our sin, wrong choices, works of the flesh and our vulnerability to the enemy. There is a way that we can be set free from all our heartache and troubles. His name is Jesus, and we can choose to come under His forgiveness, care, and protection when we, forgive others, ask Him to heal our wounds, break our vows, AND *intentionally* and *overtly* take responsibility for all the sinful attitudes in our heart that have remained by recognizing them, repenting, turning away from them and turning back to God to do things His way, all in prayer. It's not enough to just say, "Yup. Okay. I repent." You've got to get with God, one on One, be specific, open your mouth and voice your confession and repentance to Him out loud and then listen to His Spirit to direct your heart and prayer anywhere else He would want it to go. Jesus came and died, rose again and ascended to the right-hand of the Father so we could be free.

SO IF THE SON SETS YOU FREE, YOU WILL BE FREE INDEED (JOHN 8:36 ESV)

Before we pray this through, I want you to do some reflection about how you really feel and felt regarding your childhood and how you were parented.

I have a good friend who always reminds us that no one can *make* us feel anything, but I would say, no one *should* be able to make us feel anything because we *should* be allowing *only* God and His opinion about us to rule, but of course when we are children and immature, we take our cues from others—from their words to us, about us, over us, and their actions toward us speak louder than the truth. We don't even know the truth about ourselves when we're little, so yes, we very much allow others to make us feel certain ways. For example, my father physically abused me at times, and this made me feel like he didn't love me. It made me feel afraid of him and it made me feel insecure in who I was.

It goes the other way too. In fact, the five *love* languages[23] that we've all heard about, are all about how people make us feel loved by how they treat us and how they speak to us. If someone can make us feel loved by what they say and do, they can certainly speak other languages through their actions. But, yes, it is up to us as *mature adults* to discern that when others treat us poorly, it's not because there is something wrong with us. It's because there is something wrong with them. Regardless, I would venture to say that the child inside most of us is wounded in some way and we need healing.

I would encourage you to sit down by yourself (& God) with a piece of paper and prayerfully think back to how you were negatively treated and spoken to. Write down all the negative ways it made you *feel* about your home, your family, your circumstances, and yourself. This is just between you and God. It's absolutely okay for you to be completely honest with God. Ditch the whole lie that you can't be honest about this because if you are, you are being disloyal to your family and/or your parents. God does not require us to be loyal to other people to the point of covering up their sin. This is a lie. Whatever family secret you've been trying to keep, it's time to let it go and tell God about it.

After you're done writing stuff down, pray and tell God ALL about it. Pour out your heart to Him out of your mouth. It doesn't have to be loud, but you need to put actual words to it, and you need to be specific. For some it's going to be like a damn is bursting; you've held it in for so long. This might be the first time you've allowed yourself to speak about it. Take courage, my friend, you will be so much lighter when you're done.

Now, after you've told God ALL about it and admitted to Him ALL the ways you have felt in the past, pray the following prayer. I would suggest for each of the prayers you pray, read through it first so you can agree with it, then go back to the beginning and pray it with a sincere heart.

Prayer

"I now choose to forgive my parents for making me feel (speak out all the words you've written down plus any of the following that apply):

like garbage	dirty
forgotten	shameful
not wanted	angry
overlooked	fearful
invisible	ugly
anxious	unloved
unsafe	not protected
worthless	alone
embarrassed	without defense

and I give it all to You Lord. I recognize that my parents were not perfect people, just like I'm not perfect. They need Your mercy and grace just as much as I do. I choose to forgive them. Please take all these things from me now and heal all the wounds in my heart created as a result."

As you pray this, tear up the paper you wrote on into tiny pieces or put the paper in your fireplace and let it burn. Imagine giving all these things to Jesus and see Him take them and destroy them.

Secondly, forgive your parents for the negative ways in which they treated you (prayer below).

A few pages back I pointed out that raising children is a sacrifice. They take a lot of time, energy, and resources and sometimes it's difficult for us to *want* to make those sacrifices for our kids—sometimes it feels too heavy, and our flesh gets in the way. We want what we want for ourselves, and selfishness can cause us to feel resentful, frustrated, and angry that they require so much from us. We may have behaved this way toward our own children and our parents may have behaved this way toward us. Again, it's a chain of pain. So, let's first forgive our parents for acting this way toward us and then confess and repent for behaving this way toward our own children. I will list various things. Go through the list and make a check by the ones that apply to you and then pray the prayer outlined, like you mean it.

Prayer

"Father, I choose to forgive my parents for:
- Not wanting me
- Rejecting me
- Rejecting my gender
- Not celebrating me
- Not hearing me and not seeing me
- Not valuing who I was/am
- Harsh and unloving communication
- Being impatient
- Abusing me physically, verbally, emotionally, and/or sexually
- Trying to escape their responsibility by using alcohol and/or drugs

- Running away from their responsibilities (physically leaving the family)
- Ignoring me
- Not wanting to spend time with me
- Ignoring my physical needs
- Not connecting with my heart
- Not telling me that they love me
- Withdrawing from me emotionally
- Not being available to me emotionally and/or physically
- Ignoring/rejecting my emotional needs
- Being irritated and/or frustrated with me
- Being angry about caring for me and/or providing for my needs
- Choosing to over-work to avoid their responsibilities at home and with me
- Not creating a warm, loving environment in the home
- Expecting too much from me
- Expecting me to be perfect or not childlike
- Comparing me to others
- Putting me down verbally
- Lying to me
- Wishing I was someone else
- Wishing I was the other gender
- Judging my emotions as too much
- Teaching me to pretend that everything was okay when it wasn't
- Using me for their own gain
- Not keeping me safe

- Kicking me out of the family home before I was ready
- Shunning me emotionally
- Disowning me
- Avoiding me
- Making me responsible for their emotional well-being
- Making me responsible for the care of younger siblings beyond what was reasonable
- Not understanding me or my experience
- Leaving me to deal with my emotions alone
- Refusing to play with me
- Being cold, angry, and controlling
- Using fear and intimidation to control me
- Not allowing me to make mistakes
- Giving parental authority to others
- Pawning me off on others because they didn't want to look after me
- Leaving me with babysitters too much
- Leaving me alone by myself when I was too young
- not limiting my screen time and/or using an electronic device like a babysitter
- Not giving me affection
- Teaching me that I had to earn love and affection
- Causing me to doubt God's ability to love me, care for me and provide for me
- Causing my view of God to be distorted
- Not teaching me how to resolve conflict in a healthy way
- Not teaching me about Jesus, Who He is and what He did for me

- Overprotecting me
- Not allowing me to grow up and mature properly
- Not teaching me healthy responsibility
- Being jealous of me
- Trying to be God in my life
- Imposing rigid structures and rules on me

I choose to forgive my parents for all these things, and I release them fully to You God. I repent for hanging onto anger for all these years. (If *as a child* you treated your parents badly in response to their mistreatment, confess your sinful response to God now and ask for His forgiveness. Then, forgive yourself.) Lord, I confess that in response to my parents' mistreatment, I sinned against my parents by .... (be specific). I repent. Please forgive me. I choose to forgive myself and I accept Your forgiveness, God. Thank You."

Now, go back through the list and using a different color pen, check the ones that you are guilty of in the treatment of your own children and adapt them to your prayer. If you've had an abortion or in any way tried to cause the spontaneous miscarriage of any of your children, please include it in the following prayer.

Prayer

"Lord, I confess that I am guilty of mistreating my own children in the following ways . . . (read the ones that apply from the previous list changing the pronoun accordingly and add anything I have missed). I repent and I choose to forgive myself for harming my own children in these ways. Please forgive me Lord. Based on 1 John 1:9 that says, if we confess our sin to You that You are faithful and just to forgive us and purify us from all unrighteousness, I receive Your forgiveness in its fullness. I trust Your Word to be true. Thank You, God. I renounce all these behaviors, and I revoke every agreement I have unknowingly made with demons by participating in these ungodly behaviors and the harm of children. In Jesus' name, amen." *(Deliverance connected to this will be handled at the end.)

Okay, you've dealt with your stuffed emotions, forgiven your parents, repented for your childhood reactive sin, and your own sin in how you've treated your own kids. Way to go! Now, let's pray through the sinful attitudes toward your parents that you're still hanging onto as an adult. Yes, I'm going to walk you through, so you don't miss a thing. First, I will outline the steps and then give a prayer beginning at step two that you can personalize to yourself.

Step one: Praise God and thank Him for Who He is. Adoration is always a good opener in any prayer.

Step two: Confess.

Step three: Repent and ask for forgiveness.

Step four: Forgive yourself and accept God's forgiveness.

Step five: Renounce the promise or vow you made to yourself and renounce the heart attitudes you're guilty of. Then command them to go.

Prayer

"Father, I confess that I have walked in agreement with:

1. Dishonor toward my parents
2. Anger toward my parents
3. Hate toward my parents
4. Bitterness toward my parents
5. Unforgiveness toward my parents
6. Judgement toward my parents
7. Pride and independence
8. And in sin, I have promised myself that I would never/always .... (state the promise you made)."

Lord, I repent. Please forgive me for all these attitudes and for my arrogance in thinking I was able to be a good parent in my own strength.

Lord, I choose to forgive myself and I receive Your forgiveness in full. (Give yourself a moment and feel the fullness of this before moving on. Repeat it if you think you need to.)

Lord, I renounce the promise that I would never/always...... (repeat the promise word for word). I break the power of those words, and I command them to fall to the ground now.

I renounce dishonor, anger, hate, bitterness, and unforgiveness toward my parents. I renounce bitter judgements against my parents, and I renounce pride, independence and arrogance.

I bind and I COMMAND every spirit of dishonor, anger, hate, bitterness, unforgiveness, bitter judgement, pride, independence and arrogance to leave me now, in Jesus' mighty name! Go to the feet of Jesus, now! (Breathe deep and believe in faith that these spirits are leaving on your natural breathing. Repeat the command for them to leave as many times as you sense is necessary. Pray with authority, like you mean it.) Father, fill me with Your Spirit afresh again. I want to overflow with You. I receive Your filling and Your anointing now, in Jesus' name, amen."

If you find yourself coughing, yawning, crying or even burping etc. don't be alarmed. This is normal. This is deliverance. If there is no manifestation, that is fine too; this is *not* an indication that they are not leaving. Ask the Holy Spirit to give you the discernment you need.

If at any point you sense the demons are not leaving or they are causing you grief in some way, back off from commanding them to leave and just breathe for a few minutes. Thank God for His peace. Breathe and calm down, then ask the Lord what is allowing them to remain. Is there something more you need to repent for? Or someone else you need to forgive? Your children perhaps? Is there someone else you've been bitter toward? A sibling? An uncle? A grandparent? Has someone in the family offended you? If so, you must forgive them and let go of the offense. Ask the Holy Spirit to show you. When He does, go back to prayer and do the work you need to, then, command the demons again to leave you.

Let's also kick out any demon that might be attached to the sinful ways you have treated your own children which we have already confessed and renounced above:

Prayer

"Father, I have already acknowledged the ways in which I have mistreated my own children, and I repent (if you remember something else, confess it here and repent again). I bind, renounce and break covenant with every demon associated with the mistreatment of children including: the demon of violence, lust for power, lust for importance, lust for status, abuse, murder, hate of children, bitterness toward children, frustration, hard-heartedness, self-importance, self-exultation, self-centeredness, self-preservation, self-sufficiency, selfish ambition, pride, haughtiness and arrogance. I bind all these demons; I shut their mouths, and I forbid their maneuvers against me in Jesus' name. I COMMAND them all to leave me now! I command violence, lust for power, lust for importance, lust for status, abuse, murder, hate of children, bitterness toward children, frustration, hard-heartedness, self-importance, self-exultation, self-centeredness, self-preservation, self-sufficiency, selfish ambition, pride, haughtiness and arrogance to loose me now in Jesus' mighty name! Go! Get out now and go to the feet of Jesus! (Breathe deep and in faith believe that the demons are leaving you upon your natural breathing. Continue to command them to go until you sense a release.) Father, fill me completely with Your Spirit again, Amen."

If you find you are struggling to pray the prayers or to let go and forgive others or yourself, ask a *mature* Christian friend, or your pastor to help, agree, support and encourage you through it.

If you want your parenting journey to get easier, you MUST get through these prayers successfully and sincerely. You will not be able to fake your way through and see results. These doors and access points for the enemy must be closed now, before you proceed any further with this material. You ARE able with God's help to do this. He has given you His Spirit to fill you and empower you.

HE WHO IS IN YOU IS GREATER THAN HE WHO IS IN THE WORLD (1 JOHN 4:4B).

CLEANSING YOUR SPIRITUAL HOUSE

First, I want to say, "Way to go!" If you've come this far, I know you're invested in the process. I know it can be difficult to dig up stuff in your heart that you prefer to leave buried. Unfortunately, freedom, peace, and health are not found by leaving buried toxic emotions or demons in any part of our being. Rest assured, your hard work and perseverance will pay off in the end.

This chapter may be long as we're going to deal with seven pitfalls we may be ensnared by or trapped in. In the next section of the book, we are going to stand in Christ and take authority over demons, on behalf of our children, and we won't be able to do that if we are agreeing with them in our own lives. We want to make sure we close all access points the enemy may be taking advantage of in our own soul.

The Orphan Spirit

Starting off strong, let's identify what the orphan spirit is, what it does and how it gets in.

Satan's number one goal is to drive a wedge between us and God and prevent us from accepting and experiencing our new identity as a child of God, in His perfect family. The devil attempts to keep us in old patterns of thinking, perhaps continuing to expect the same old way we've experienced family in the past.

The orphan spirit is a demon entity that attaches to us when we experience dysfunctional family life where we do not attach emotionally to our parents in a healthy way, and we agree with other destructive things like shame, self-hate, and rejection. We believe lies like, *I'm not loved, I'm rejected, I don't belong, I'm not good enough, I'm alone,* and *no one will ever love me*. And it seems that everywhere we turn, things happen that reinforce these lies.

What are some of the symptoms of orphan living? They can be (mark the ones you see in yourself):

- Being fiercely independent (self-reliant, hardheaded, stubborn)
- Feeling like you don't belong
- Searching desperately for connection in others and even things
- Fear of the future
- Fear of lack
- Fear of poverty
- Fear of intimacy
- Fear of rejection

- Fear of being alone
- Jealous of others
- Living in lack in various ways including financially
- Hoarding
- Stinginess
- Striving incessantly for everything
- Performance mentality
- Workaholism
- Lack of peace
- Lack of security
- Self-protection
- Feeling ashamed
- Hating oneself
- Rejecting oneself
- Self-deprecation
- Pattern of rejection from others

Freedom From the Orphan Spirit

So, on our journey to get free from the orphan spirit, we first need to tackle some lesser demons that are connected like shame, self-hate, rejection, fear, and whatever else is related to the above list of symptoms. We are going to tackle shame first.

Shame

If you struggle with feeling ashamed, what reason in your mind, do you have for being ashamed?

Sexual abuse? If you were abused sexually, I am truly sorry. My heart goes out to you. Please see someone—a pastor, or trusted prayer minister who is equipped in deliverance ministry for help. Sexual abuse requires deliverance from more than we can handle in this book and more than you can handle on your own. I do invite you, however, into releasing the shame you may feel from it.

When we are abused sexually as children, we may feel like somehow it is our fault. We must completely reject this lie. A child is never responsible for the sexual abuse they have suffered. It was solely the responsibility of the adult(s) to put an end to it and remove you from that situation—to protect you. We must NOT put unrealistic expectations on the child within ourselves.

When sexual abuse happens to a child, a child does not understand that what is happening is wrong. Something may feel *off* in their spirit, but to all the fleshly senses, it can feel right. Confusion swirls. Sometimes, it simply *feels* like someone is loving them and what could be wrong about that? Please do not accept shame. You were manipulated, groomed, and coerced by a twisted perverted spirit operating through an individual. Release yourself from the false responsibility to understand adult things when you were a child.

In the previous chapter, we talked about forgiveness briefly. Based on Matthew 6:14-15, if we want to be forgiven, we must forgive others. This includes everyone, no matter how heinous their crime. Understandably, sexual abuse is very traumatizing, but it is not an exception to the requirement of God. We must forgive.

Beloved, I know it's difficult. Please ask the Holy Spirit to help you—to help you even have the desire to forgive. Please take as much time as you need to process this through. Don't rush yourself. But also, don't skip over it. (If you feel you need to come back to it after you receive ministry from someone, please do that.)

In addition to forgiving your perpetrator(s), you may also need to forgive a parent for not intervening; you may also need to forgive God. Have you ever wondered why He allowed it or didn't protect you?

I'm sorry if it feels like I'm moving too fast. Take a break if you need to. Breathe. Connect with God for a moment and let Him love you. Perhaps listen to a worship song or two. Whatever you need to do to connect with the Spirit. Remember that you are loved, and you can do all things through Him Who gives you strength. Also remember that God wants to heal everything in your heart that needs healing and when we cooperate with Him, no pain you've been through will be left unredeemed or wasted. Every trauma and hurtful thing will be turned around in God's hands and the devil will rue the day he ever messed with you. Your best revenge against the devil is to cooperate with God, forgive those who hurt you, and allow God to fully heal you.

And on your behalf, right now, I bind and shut down the spirit of unforgiveness, rejection, offense, and trauma that may be resisting you right now. I command them to cease and desist their maneuvers against you, in Jesus' name. You are free to follow the Lord in His directives and desires for your life.

You are loved and you are the beloved of the Lord.

YOU CAN DO ALL THINGS THROUGH CHRIST WHO GIVES YOU STRENGTH

Holy Spirit, lead us into ALL truth!

You, my friend, are more than a conqueror through Christ who loves you. Nothing has the power to separate you from the love of God!

> For I am convinced that neither death nor life, neither angels nor demons, neither the present nor the future, nor any powers, neither height nor depth, nor anything else in all creation, will be able to separate us from the love of God that is in Christ Jesus our Lord (Romans 8:38-39 NIV).

So, why didn't God intervene? Beloved, He tried. I'm certain of it. God pulled out all the stops and tried to steer that person away from violating you, but when people are oppressed by perverted sexual demons, especially when they aren't saved, they can't hear God. I believe God would have caused other things to happen to try and avert the situation, like making the phone ring, or causing a distraction of some kind, but sometimes perpetrators are hell bent and demonically motivated. God was there with you, and He cried with you. He then put into motion His plan to draw you to Himself, to save you, heal you, and redeem your pain. Jesus is very possessive of you; He vowed that He would make you shine and never let you go.

When you are ready, pray something like this:

> "Lord, You know the heartache I endured. You know the sin committed against me. You were there. And I'm sorry for being angry with You for allowing it to happen. I understand that You are always for me, working on my behalf and protecting

me as far as You are able. I also know that the adults in my life should have done their part in protecting me. Right now, I choose to forgive You, Lord, and I choose to forgive every adult in my life that did not protect me as they should have. And as an act of my will, I choose to forgive... (say your perpetrator's name) for... (name their crime). Help me Jesus to make this decision to forgive, every single day, until my heart catches up with my mind. I renounce the lie that it was my fault. I renounce the lie that I should be ashamed of myself. I renounce the lie that... (renounce whatever other lie you think you have believed). I repent for thinking less of myself because of this. And I repent for allowing this to steal my dignity, confidence, and love for myself. I repent for walking in agreement with shame. I renounce shame right now in Jesus' name and I command it to go from me now. Shame, you will go to the feet of Jesus. (Breathe deep believing in faith that it is leaving on your natural breathing. Continue to command it to go until you sense a release.) Father, heal every wound in my heart created by these events and fill me up completely with Your Spirit. Amen."

For our purposes right now, we are only dealing with shame. As I said earlier, please get help from a ministry partner to be delivered from other things, such as trauma, fear related to the events, lust, perversion, man-hating spirit, woman-hating spirit, worthlessness, hatred, and any type of sexually deviant spirit. Yes, there *can* be a lot.

If you don't have anyone in your church or geographical region who can assist you, please send an email to barbaradesimon@gmail.com explaining who you are and what you need. I will let you know if I can meet with you in person or on Zoom for prayer-ministry.

If you are ashamed of something you did in your past, pray:

> "Father, I confess that I ...... (name your sin). I am sorry. Please forgive me. I choose to forgive myself and (Name anyone else involved. Anyone who may have pressured you into it or participated with you). I receive Your forgiveness now, in Jesus' name. Lord, heal every wound in me that caused me to act out in this way and heal every wound in me this has created. I renounce and break agreement with shame right now and I command it to leave me now, in Jesus' name. Go! You will leave on my natural breathing right now and you will go to the feet of Jesus. (Breathe deep and continue to command it to go until you sense a release.) Father, fill me up with Your Spirit. In Jesus' name, amen."

If you're not sure why you feel ashamed, ask the Lord to show you. Then simply follow the pattern in the previous prayers. Forgive anyone who may have made you feel that way. Come out of agreement with shame, renounce it, and command it to go from you, in Jesus' name.

Self-hate, and rejection is dealt with in a similar fashion. Once you identify that you have felt hate for yourself, pray something like this:

> "Lord, I confess that I have hated myself. I am sorry and I repent. (be specific if you know you have

hated certain things about yourself). I choose to forgive myself for ……. And I receive Your forgiveness, Lord. I release myself from self-hate in Jesus' name. I renounce self-hate and I command it to leave me now, in Jesus' name. Self-hate, go! Get out and go to the feet of Jesus. (Again, breathe deep and continue to command it to leave until you sense a release. The Lord may show you specific things that caused you to hate yourself and if He does, pray through these things.) Lord, fill me up with Your Spirit. In Jesus' name, amen."

Rejection

Rejection is a big one. So much can happen to us that causes us to feel rejected. But rejection is actually a lie. We are not rejected—maybe by people at times, but never by God and that is all that matters. God has accepted us and bought us with the very blood of His Son. Here's a truth bomb for you:

IF WE ALLOW REJECTION TO DEFINE US, WE HAVE DECIDED TO VALUE ACCEPTANCE BY PEOPLE OVER THE ACCEPTANCE OF GOD.

Yikes! Don't do it! This is idolatry my friend. God's acceptance of us should be and needs to be the only acceptance that truly matters to us. Who can reject who God has accepted? Think about it. God has already decided that you ARE worthy! Believe it despite what others say and do. If someone rejects you, that's their problem; they simply are not able to see your worth. Maybe God doesn't want them in your life for a reason.

Prayer

"Lord, I repent for walking in agreement with rejection. And I repent for rejecting myself. Please forgive me. I choose right now to forgive every person who has ever rejected me. (If you think of specific examples, name them.) I choose to forgive ...... for ...... I choose to forgive myself for rejecting myself. Thank You for Your forgiveness, Lord; I receive it now in its fullness. Father, heal every wound in me that was created by rejection and that caused me to feel rejected. I renounce rejection and I command it to go from me now, in Jesus' name. Rejection, go! I'm done with you. Leave me now and go to the feet of Jesus. (Breathe deep and continue to command it to go until you sense that it's gone.) Fill me up with Your Spirit, Lord. In Jesus' name, amen."

Fear and Other Symptoms

Finally, pray through the other symptoms of the orphan spirit you identified in yourself back on page 141 and 142.

Prayer

"Father, forgive me for being hardheaded, stubborn, self-reliant, stingy, addicted to work, and jealous. Forgive me, God, for walking in agreement with a spirit of self-protection and fear—specifically the fear of the future, the fear of lack, the fear of intimacy, fear of rejection, and the fear of being alone. Forgive me, God, for hoarding, striving, and walking in a performance mentality trying to earn love. I renounce all these behaviors. I renounce striving, stinginess, workaholism, self-protection, stubbornness, jealousy, and performance and I renounce the spirit of fear and the orphan spirit right now, in Jesus' name. I command the spirit of jealousy, the spirit of fear, and the orphan spirit to leave me right now, in Jesus' name. Go! Come out upon my natural breathing and go to the feet of Jesus. (Breathe deep and continue to command these spirits to leave until you sense they have gone.) I thank You, God, that I have been adopted into Your family. Forgive me for not living like a true son/daughter. Thank You for Your forgiveness, God. Help me to receive You as my good, good Father and understand Your love for me. Fill me afresh with Your Spirit. In Jesus' name, amen."

Anger and Frustration with Our Kids

I don't think I need to explain this one; you know exactly what I'm talking about. In an effort to keep this book short, let's pray.

Prayer

"Father, I confess that I have been holding anger and frustration toward my children in my heart because of their behaviors toward me and others. Please forgive me. I choose right now to forgive my children for: (list their bad behaviors and be specific). I release them to You, God. I renounce anger and frustration toward my children, and I command anger and frustration toward my children to leave me now, in Jesus' name. Go! Loose me now and go to the feet of Jesus, right now! (Breathe deep and in faith believe that these spirits are leaving on your natural exhale.) Lord, heal every wound in me that was created by their behaviour and fill me afresh with Your Spirit, in Jesus' name. Amen."

Unmet Expectations

Most of us have expectations don't we, when we go into marriage and have children? We expect our husband or wife to be a certain way, and we expect our children to act a certain way. We are raised with certain customs and traditions, and we just expect that they will continue in our own family. Inevitably though, we end up being disappointed about something because our expectations are not met. This can cause anger and resentment to build up and really get under our skin.

When my husband and I started to have children, I expected that we would go to firework displays, and parades, and go camping as a family because that is what my childhood family did. I never thought my family would be any different. But it turned out that my husband hates crowds, and he didn't want to do ANY of those activities. It was a real let down and I had to forgive him for not meeting my expectations whilst letting go of other expectations of him as well.

Did you expect to have the million-dollar family—one boy and one girl—well-behaved, angelic like offspring who were obedient and smart? Or did you expect something else? Did you expect parenting to be easier? Did you expect it to be fun, not exasperating? Think about it for a few minutes.

Get a piece of paper out and jot down your answers to:

What are you disappointed about?

Are your disappointments related to unmet expectations?

Write down your disappointments and their corresponding unmet expectations.

Here's a big one in marriage: "I feel disappointed that my husband doesn't love me the way I want to be loved or the way I can receive it best." This is very common, and I have been there. Unfortunately, some men are not wired to love in certain ways and the Lord wants us to release them from the expectations that they can't seem to meet.

Perhaps the Lord will do a work in your husband's heart to empower him to do what he can't in his own strength but it's not up to us, as wives, to require it from him or to try to change him into what we want. It's time to release our husband to the Lord so He can do what He wants to do in them. In the meantime, wives, let's pursue the Lord with all our heart and allow Him to pour into us His love. Let's let God fill our cup so we are not left wanting anymore. I invite you to pray through this now.

Prayer

"Lord, I confess that I have been disappointed with (or about)......

I thought it would be different. I expected that ....

I choose to forgive.......... (forgive anyone who you see as having caused disappointment) for ....

I ask You, God, to heal my heart of the pain and the sting of all these unmet expectations.

I release my expectations of .... to You, God, and I accept him/her for who he/she is, just as he/she is, faults and all.

Father, heal every wound in my heart created by disappointment and unmet expectations.

I come out of agreement with disappointment and all unmet expectations right now, in Jesus' name. I renounce them and I command them to leave me now. Disappointment and unmet expectations, go! Get out and go to the feet of Jesus. (Breathe deep and believe in faith that these spirits are leaving on your natural breathing.)

Lord, fill me up with Your Spirit, in Jesus' name. Amen."

Words and Curses

Proverbs 18:20-21 says this:

> From the fruit of their mouth a person's stomach is filled; with the harvest of their lips they are satisfied. The tongue has the power of life and death, and those who love it will eat its fruit (NIV).

Pertaining to our words, I believe there are three areas where we get in trouble:

I. The words that we speak in anger or exasperation toward our children, perhaps derogatory names or phrases like, "you're driving me nuts," or "you're a pain in the neck." What about other derogatory phrases that you perhaps meant as a joke but hurt them regardless? For example, my father said to me several times, "You make a good-looking boy," or "a blind man would be glad to see it," (referring to my new haircut). My mom always had my hair cut super short when I was young as it was curly, thick, and course and she didn't know what to do with it. My dad thought he was being funny, but I wasn't laughing.

II. The words we have used to speak about our kids to others. Have you used words like: "My kids are angry, defiant, unmanageable, unhinged, feral, wild, hyper, disrespectful, bad, etc.?

III. Believing and speaking that this generation *as a whole* is out of control, defiant, unmanageable, feral, defiant, disrespectful, entitled. etc. What descriptions of this generation have you heard and agreed with? Make a note of it and renounce it in the prayer coming up.

Prayer

"Father, forgive me for saying to (say their name), (repeat what you said). Forgive me for calling (say their name), a (say the name you called him/her). I renounce all these words in Jesus' name, and I break their power. Father, forgive me for agreeing with the lie that this generation of kids is: ... (repeat what you agreed with). I renounce this lie in Jesus' name and I break the power of my words. Forgive me, God, for enacting curses against my children and the children of this generation with my words. I choose to forgive myself and I receive Your forgiveness in its fullness. Heal every wound in me,

God, that caused me to speak in this way. Thank You, Jesus, Amen"

Involvement in the Occult and Yoga

In this section, we will repent for participating in any religion or religious practice that is *rooted* in any religion other than Christianity, including man-made traditions, that are not biblical, from Roman Catholicism, including praying to Mary and other saints, and worshipping Mary and including any participation in the occult.

I include Yoga because Yoga originated in the spiritual practices of Hinduism and Buddhism. Yoga means yoke or union, so when you do Yoga, you are joining yourself with a demonic deity. Yes, I know that there are versions of Yoga that don't focus on the spiritual side of things, but many poses in Yoga are named after and represent Hindu and Yogic deities (false gods or demons). Here's a quote from a website about Yoga:

> "As a way of connecting to, revering and paying respect to deities, many yoga postures represent not just what the deity looks like, but also everything they stand for. As we practise the posture, we put our focus on the energy and essence of the deity and look to embody their qualities."[24]

If that doesn't creep you out, I don't know what will.

Here's the definition of Yoga from Wikipedia:

> "Yoga is a group of physical, mental, and spiritual practices or disciplines that originated in ancient India, aimed at controlling body and mind to attain

various salvation goals, as practiced in the Hindu, Jain, and Buddhist traditions."

Did you catch that last part? "Controlling body and mind to attain various salvation goals." Friend, you're already saved. Don't mess with it by practicing Yoga.

Do you remember in the Bible how Jesus talks about how a good tree produces good fruit and a bad tree produces bad fruit? He's talking about people, but the principle can be applied to other things. If the root of something is bad, all the fruit on that tree will be bad. It doesn't matter how you attempt to alter the fruit. You can polish it up and make it shiny, it doesn't remove the bad from it because it came from a bad root. The roots of all Yoga are bad, my friend. Maybe for someone who practices Hinduism or Buddhism, it's fine, but you're not Hindus or Buddhist. Right? So don't pay homage to their gods. This is idolatry. The very first commandment in the Bible says, "Thou shalt have no other gods before me (Exodus 20:3 KJV)." Period. (See this article for more information: https://www.thetruelight.net/wp/10-yoga-poses-that-offer-worship-to-hindu-deities/)

Before we begin in prayer, put a tick beside all the occult practices, games, cults, secret societies, and alternative healing modalities (rooted in other religious or New Age beliefs) you or your ancestors have been involved in:

Manifesting	Palm reading	Tarot cards
Ouija board	Magic Eight Ball	Zodiac signs
Psychic readings	Astrology	Numerology
Hypnosis	Astral Projection	Clairvoyance
Magic (black & white)	Automatic Writing	Table lifting
Séance	Levitation	Telepathy

Divination   Spirit guides   Blood pacts
Fetishism   Horoscopes   Wicca
Qabalah   Rosicrucianism   Spiritualism
Theosophy   Anthroposophy   New Age
Hermetic Order of the Golden Dawn   Reiki
Healing crystals   Hypnosis   Energy healing
Dry needling   Acupuncture   Scientology
Christian Science   Witness Lee   Hare Krishna
Ancient Chinese Medicine   Jehovah's Witness
The Way International   Unification Church
Unitarian/Universalist Church   Mormonism
Church of the Living Word   Theosophical Society
The Bahá'í Faith   Children of God
Swedenborgian Church   Roman Catholicism
Grace Communion Int. (Worldwide Church of God)
Job's Daughters   Shriners
Freemasonry[44]   Orange Order
Any fraternity or sorority

Before you pray, gather any paraphernalia that you have associated with these religions and practices like Tarot cards, potions, and books and destroy them. Do not give them away as we don't want anyone else to be deceived by them either. If you can't bring yourself to do it before prayer, do it after.

Prayer

"Father, forgive me for participating in:
(list all the things you checked off from the list)
I am truly sorry for my idolatrous behavior. I repent. I choose to forgive myself and every person

---

[44] Please see appendix A for a prayer to be free from Freemasonry in particular.

who participated with me or encouraged me to do so. I renounce all these practices, false religions, every lie, every vow taken, and every demon associated with them. And I ask You, God, to deliver me from every one. (If you can specifically remember any of the vows you took for the secret societies, sorority or fraternity, renounce them here) I renounce the vow that...... (Please see Appendix A for a prayer to renounce Freemasonry.)

I bind and renounce the spirits of error, deception, confusion, and antichrist, in Jesus' name. I command every spirit that has gained access to me through any of these practices and religions to leave me now, in Jesus' name and I command the spirits of error, deception, confusion, and antichrist to leave me now, in Jesus' name. Go to the feet of Jesus! (Breathe and continue to command them to go until you sense it is done.)

Father, forgive me for practicing Yoga. Forgive me for paying homage to false gods through the movements of my body. I repent for using my body as an instrument of unrighteousness. Forgive me for worshipping other gods.

I choose to forgive myself, every Yoga instructor, and every person who participated with me or led me into it. I receive Your forgiveness, Lord.

I renounce idolatry and false worship. I bind and renounce every deity associated with Yoga including Lakshmi, Saraswati, Durga, Hanuman, Dancing Shiva, Chakrasamvara, Hevajra,

Kalachakra, Krishna, Radha, Shiva, Ganesha, Vishnu, Brahma, Kali, Parvati, Mahakala, and Tara. I bind and renounce the eight limbs of Yoga, and the Kundalini spirit. I renounce every Yoga pose and move I have done. I ask You, Lord, to deliver me from each one right now. I command every one of these false gods and their demons to leave me right now, in Jesus' name! Go! Leave me now and go to the feet of Jesus. (Breathe. Continue to command them to go until you sense that you are free. Envision them leaving upon your natural breathing.) Thank You, Jesus. Fill me with Your Spirit afresh. In Jesus' name, amen."

Sexual Sin

The only sex that is sanctioned by God is regular sex between a husband and a wife, not including anal sex or oral sex. Oral and anal sex are both perversions of sex to accommodate for homosexuality. Although we love people who identify as other sexual orientations, we do not support the acts of other sexual orientations, including homosexuality, because God does not condone it (see Romans 1:24-27). Sex before marriage is fornication and considered a sin (Galatians 5:19). Just because certain actions are accepted by society, doesn't mean it's holy. As Christians, holiness is our plumb line. We don't compare ourselves to one another, we compare ourselves to God to know where we stand.

Make a mental note which of the following sexual perversions you've participated in and renounce them in the prayer:

fornication (sex before marriage)   homosexuality

sodomy (anal sex/oral sex)	adultery
compulsive masturbation	pedophilia
sadomasochism	bestiality
voyeurism	pornography
incest	fantasy

Prayer

"Father, forgive me for participating in the following sexual sin: (name the ones you are guilty of). Forgive me, God, for using my body as an instrument of unrighteousness. I choose to forgive myself and I choose to forgive (name your partners) for participating with me. I choose to forgive .... for pressuring me into it (if this applies) and/or taking advantage of me. Lord, I receive Your forgiveness. Please heal the wounds in my heart that caused me to act out in sexual dysfunction, to seek out attention in this way before marriage and to allow others to take advantage of me. I renounce the spirit of lust, perversion, and rebellion in Jesus' name. (Also renounce the spirits of the perversions you've participated in. For example: I renounce the spirit of homosexuality, the spirit of fornication, the spirit of sodomy etc.) And I command the spirits of lust, perversion, and........ (name all the other spirits you renounced) to leave me right now, in Jesus' name. Go! Come out and go to the feet of Jesus. (Breathe deep and in faith believe that these spirits are coming out upon your exhale. Continue to command them to go until you sense freedom.) Lord, I ask that You cleanse my blood line, up and down, from these spirits. Thank You, Jesus. Fill me afresh with Your Spirit. Amen."

Soul Ties

A soul tie is a strong emotional connection and reliance on someone or something to help us feel better. It is someone or something that we look to in order to get our emotional needs met. Very often a soul tie is the reason for an addiction. The term "soul tie" is not in the Bible, but the issue with them is actually idolatry.

We were meant to get our emotional needs met primarily by God, but we end up seeking out lesser lovers here on earth that we can see and feel because it's easier and we want a quick fix.

A soul tie can be created with things like video games or their characters if they somehow feed our emotions by making us feel powerful, or perhaps because of the adrenaline or dopamine that is produced in us by them.

A soul tie can be created with pets if we become too attached to them. Soul ties can also be created between friends if we become too reliant on them for our emotional well being.

Soul ties are created between a mother and her babies which is healthy when they are young, but the mom must let them go gradually and allow them to grow up, becoming their own person. There may come a time, when your children are older, when you will need to cut your soul tie with them, through prayer, so they can be free to become all they need to be and were created to be—or so they can stop hanging onto you in dependency that is unhealthy. I've also seen mothers who need to cut a soul tie with their prodigal child so that they (the mom) can live in peace. A soul tie between two adults that is unhealthy ends up working like puppet strings, exerting control over the other.

Lastly, a soul tie is created between sexual partners, every single time. So, each partner you've had, you have a soul tie with, and it could be causing mayhem in your marriage; you may still have feelings for them, and you can't seem to stop thinking about them. The demons that are oppressing your previous partner, could be oppressing you too simply because you have a soul tie with that demonized person. So, let's break soul ties, with sexual partners first.

Prayer

"Father, forgive me for creating ungodly soul ties and covenants with people through sex who are not my spouse. I repent. Please forgive me, God. I choose to forgive... (name each person by name if you can), and I choose to forgive myself for seeking this ungodly union. Lord, I receive Your forgiveness and confess that I am forgiven. I now break and renounce ungodly soul ties, unions, covenants, and influences in body, soul and spirit, with .... (name each partner). I release .... (name each partner) back to You God, to heal and restore. I send back to them now, washed in Your blood, the piece of their heart wrongly attached to me, and I ask that You heal every wound in their heart that caused them to seek out our union. I take and receive back to me the piece of my heart wrongly attached to them, washed in Your blood, and I ask You, God, to heal every wound in my heart that caused me to seek out our union. I now break and cancel every transference from their bloodline to mine and every curse empowered through our sin. I cut every transference and curse off of my life, body, soul, marriage, family, children, destiny, and future that came from them, in Jesus' name. Lord, cleanse my blood through the generations forward and back, in Jesus' name. Thank You for healing me. Fill me again with Your Spirit. Amen."

Now, let's identify what else you may have a soul tie with that is ungodly. Spend a few minutes in prayer and ask the Holy Spirit to show you. It could be anything you can't seem to say, "No" to. Or anything you are addicted to (even food, like sugar or video games). Write them down. After you've got them written down, ask yourself and the Holy Spirit, "What does this thing or person do for me?" "How does it (or they) make me feel?" "What am I relying on it for?" Now ask yourself, "How can I get that same need met in a godly way?" (Adapt the following prayer as needed.)

Prayer

"Father, forgive me for relying on and creating a soul tie with...

Forgive me for looking to this to feel better or to feel...

Help me to rely on You, God. Help me to look to You. I repent for idolatrous behavior and for replacing You with other things and people. I choose to forgive myself and I receive Your forgiveness. (*If your soul tie is with another person:* I choose to forgive .... for their cooperation in our ungodly union.) I now break and renounce every ungodly soul tie, union, covenant, and influence in body, soul and spirit, with ………… (name each thing or person). (*If the soul tie is with another person:* I send back to ……… the piece of their heart wrongly attached to me. Wash it in Your blood, Lord, and heal every wound in their heart that caused them to cooperate in a co-dependant relationship.) I take and receive back to me the piece of my heart that I surrendered to (person or thing) washed in Your blood, and I ask You, God, to heal every wound in my heart that caused me to rely on anything or anyone other than You. Fill every whole in my heart with Your love and fill me with Your peace. (If applicable) I release to You all trauma, stress, and anxiety I have been cooperating with and trying to medicate with ……… Heal me, Lord. I choose to trust You and rely on You. I bind and renounce every spirit of addiction, and I command it to leave me now, in Jesus' name. I bind and renounce idolatry and I command it to leave me now, in Jesus' name. Addiction and idolatry, go now! Go to the feet of Jesus and never come back. (Breathe deep and in faith believe that these spirits are leaving your body on your exhale.) Fill me with Your Spirit, Lord. In Jesus' name, amen."

Now, are there any friendships you need to step back from? Are there any food items you need to purge from your fridge or pantry? Are there any TV programs you need to stop watching? Any games you need to stop playing?

Way to go friend. You're doing great!

These have been the seven major areas that the Lord put on my heart to assist you in cleaning up before you attempt to stand against spirits harassing your kids. We need to be fortified first, then we can be a united front for them.

UNITED WE STAND

You're almost there my friends. I know it might be tiring emotionally, but boy oh boy are you going to be set up for success. In this second to last chapter of this section, we're going to talk about unity, roles and responsibilities in marriage, and touch on forgiveness again. As parents, we need to stand as a united front.

So, I don't know if you know this, but marriage is hard. Or is it just me? No? Okay, so each partner has their own ideas as to how things should be done, how money is spent, and how to split the chores at home and with the kids. Right? Whose night is it to do the baths? Who's morning is it to get the kids off to school?

There's a lot on our plate and many times it takes a compromise to survive and stay in some semblance of peace. Sometimes we need to concede to the other and let the other win. We need to pick our battles. Right? Some things are deal breakers and others aren't. Can we agree that we're going to do all we must to recover as a family? Whatever it takes? Sometimes it takes a real, gut-level conversation with one another about what's been silently chipping away at our peace and love for one another.

I know that you all don't do this 'cause y'all marriages are golden, but sometimes married people let things slide that probably shouldn't be allowed to slide, and sometimes they sweep things under the rug when probably the things should just be cleaned up properly the first time. How do I know this? I've done it. Yup, that's me. Miss. Peacekeeper. Just keep'n the peace so we can all get through life. The problem with this is it makes us bitter and sometimes sick.

It's vital for married couples to communicate with one another—not pointing fingers, blaming the other or chastising, but communicating with love, kindness, and truth. I would suggest visiting the famous love chapter in the Bible in 1 Corinthians 13.

Starting in verse four, we learn that love is patient, kind, does not envy, does not boast, is not proud, does not dishonor, is not self-seeking, is not easily angered, keeps no record of wrongs, does not delight in evil but rejoices with the truth, always protects, always trusts, always hopes, and always perseveres. Examine yourselves, my friends. Where have you fallen short of this goal?

Communicate with your spouse, admit your shortcomings, and ask for his/her forgiveness. Be an agent of reconciliation as we are called to be. It is vital that we can stand against the wiles of the enemy for our children, united, making sure nothing is there to get in our way. Do what you can and then ask the Lord to cover the rest in His mercy.

Next, let's talk about responsibilities on both sides. First, I'm going to pick on husbands. From a biblical perspective what is a husband/father responsible for or meant to be for his family?

The Resolution for Men

Back in 2011, the Kendrick brothers released a movie called *Courageous* about four police officers who struggle with their faith and fulfilling their God-given roles as husbands and fathers. It's my favorite movie that the Kendrick brothers have released so far.

In *Courageous*, the men make resolutions to themselves and their families to honor God and fulfill their commitments and responsibilities as men, husbands, and fathers. Then, after the movie was released, the Kendrick brothers, Stephen and Alex along with Randy Alcorn encouraged men to make the same resolutions for themselves through a book called, *The Resolution for Men*. Many thoughts over the next several paragraphs are motivated from that inspiring book. I will also share the resolutions they suggest that men take; this will help us to know what a husband's/father's godly responsibility is. Everything in the resolution is inspired by biblical text.

Men were intended by God to live courageously for their faith and their family—to be the spiritual leaders of their home. Fathers were meant to "win the hearts of their children."[25] Wow. I love that. In other words, the connection between fathers and their children is *intentionally* forged rather than something that happens automatically. It is something that takes intentional focus and effort. The number one thing that every father needs to have with their children is a heart-to-heart relationship and connection.

How is a heart-to-heart connection formed? It is formed through the following:

- Communicating with your children from your heart/speaking to them and over them, heart felt words that tell them how much you love them and how special they are to you.
- Allowing them to communicate their heart to you.
- Apologizing to them if you have messed up, and asking them to forgive you.
- Modeling forgiveness.
- Modeling appropriate affection and respect to others (especially to your/his wife).
- Being the authority in the home and expressing that appropriately, without harshness.
- Keeping your cool but being firm.
- Spending time with them.
- Doing the things that they enjoy with them EVEN if you don't enjoy the activity.
- Supporting them.
- Showing up for them.
- Showing appropriate affection to them.
- Modeling the fulfillment of responsibility in your home.

I think of the verse in Ephesians 6:4 that says, "Fathers, do not exasperate your children; instead, bring them up in the training and instruction of the Lord" (NIV). The original word for exasperate also means to provoke, anger or enrage.

Ellicott's commentary on BibleHub says, "It denotes the exasperation produced by arbitrary and unsympathetic rule."[26] I believe ruling over a child unsympathetically happens in the context of a father/child relationship that is void of heart-to-heart connection. A heart-to-heart connection requires not only sympathy but also empathy.

Here's the resolution for men found in the book, *The Resolution for Men*:

> "I DO solemnly resolve before God to take full responsibility for myself, my wife, and my children.
>
> I WILL love them, protect them, serve them, and teach them the Word of God as the spiritual leader of my home.
>
> I WILL be faithful to my wife, to love and honor her, and be willing to lay down my life for her as Jesus Christ did for me.
>
> I WILL bless my children and teach them to love God with all of their hearts, all of their minds, and all of their strength.
>
> I WILL train them to honor authority and live responsibly.
>
> I WILL confront evil, pursue justice, and love mercy.
>
> I WILL pray for others and treat them with kindness, respect, and compassion.
>
> I WILL work diligently to provide for the needs of my family.

I WILL forgive those who have wronged me and reconcile with those I have wronged.

I WILL learn from my mistakes, repent for my sins, and walk with integrity as a man answerable to God.

I WILL seek to honor God, be faithful to His church, obey His Word, and do His will.

I WILL courageously work with the strength God provides to fulfill this resolution for the rest of my life and for His glory.

As for me and my house, we will serve the LORD (Joshua 24:15)."[27]

Husbands, are you convicted yet? Are you overwhelmed? If yes, I don't think you're alone. We are all human and we all have our weaknesses and triggers.

Even though you know that right now, you may not be doing a great job at fulfilling that resolution, there is hope. There is healing. And it is possible to fulfill this resolution *as the Holy Spirit enables you*, but you may need to get healed and delivered from soul wounds and ungodly heart attitudes first, as we have been doing.

One of the greatest enemies to manhood is passivity which ultimately operates in a man who lacks vision and understanding of, and belief in, their purpose and value to God, those around them, their family, community and even the world.

The Kendrick brothers say:

> "Too many men sadly waste their lives. They don't really know the God they claim to worship and have not ultimately concluded what they are living for. Halfhearted and indecisive, they spiritually wander through life in a fog of confusion and apathy. They can tell you what they're doing this weekend, but they have no clue about their purpose in life or in eternity..... At home, men are notorious for being oblivious to the huge leadership vacuum their passivity creates. They don't realize how negatively their wives and children are affected by their lack of spiritual direction and leadership."[28]

And most importantly:

> "Throughout history, men who lived incredible lives and left great legacies did it intentionally. They knew that men do not stumble upon integrity or accidentally find themselves being faithful to God. Passivity merely leads to futility. A man cannot be passive about what Scripture tells him to do for his family and expect to be found faithful to God in the end. *He must see with spiritual eyes and realize that future generations are directly impacted by his daily decisions.*"[29]

Did you catch that last sentence? Future generations are directly impacted by a father's daily decisions. In fact, passivity very often has been passed on to a man from his father who may have gotten it from his father and so on. So much of our behavior is picked up on and mimicked by our children; this is why it is so important what we model. What we do ends up being more important than what we say.

We also need to recognize where this pattern, throughout the generations, of passivity starts—not necessarily when but how. Perhaps it started with you or perhaps it started four generations ago, but it started with someone being emasculated or deprived of their masculinity, courage, and strength. In other words, they were not allowed to be a boy, or they were criticized to the point that their self-worth as a boy was stripped away—a heart-breaking scenario for sure. Again, the good news is men can be healed of the effects of this ungodly treatment.

Men can come out of passivity through prayer and by diligently seeking the Lord for His vision for his life and the empowerment to courageously follow the path God has for him.

We will pray through passivity together, but first, I'd like you to consider what effect your passivity has had on your wife and children. You probably give 100% on the job, right? Perhaps even more. And that's awesome. But you have responsibilities at home too that you can't ignore, at least not if you want to live a godly life. You must have work/home balance, as does your wife. Both parents must be doing their part at home.

If you've been passive at home, ignoring responsibility, abdicating authority, your wife feels it. It hurts her and it puts her in the difficult position of carrying a burden she was not meant to carry alone. She needs to know that she and your children are just as important to you as your work, if not more. And don't think that just verbalizing this to your wife is enough. No. You MUST act that way too. You must walk the talk. Your behavior speaks louder than your words. I'm sorry but I've got to be real here. . . if you speak it but don't prove it with your actions, you are deceived and you are not speaking truth. You don't know your own heart ("The heart is deceitful above all things, And desperately wicked; Who can know it?" (Jer.17:9 NKJV)). What you *DO* demonstrates what is *really* in your heart, not what you say.

At the end of your life it won't matter *where* you worked or how much money you made. The only things that will matter are how you loved your wife, children and others and what you did to advance the Kingdom of God. So, *right now*, let's value the right things, so we don't lose what's most important.

Unfortunately, if you've been passive, not fulfilling your role as a godly husband and father, your wife has probably reacted in ungodly ways, in anger and disrespect. Couples can end up in a *stand off* with one another, blaming each other with no one willing to take the responsibility of where the dysfunction started. And where did it start? Did you "check out" from relationship and/or your responsibilities in response to her disrespect? Or did she disrespect you in response to your "checking out?" Sometimes there's no clear answer. We just have to be willing to *exercise love* by *forgiving* the other before we receive an apology. When we forgive in advance, our heart is positioned rightly for reconciliation and willing to be the one to take responsibility first for *our* part in the conflict. Men, let's pray.

Prayer

"Father, I confess that I have been holding onto anger toward (your wife's name) for (pray all that apply):

- *Seeming* to be ungrateful for what I do

- Disrespecting me
- Dishonoring me
- Criticizing me
- Speaking hurtful words to me or about me

(Add anything else you're angry about.)

I repent. Please forgive me.

I also confess that I have been holding onto unforgiveness toward (your wife's name). I repent. Please forgive me.

I choose to forgive (your wife's name) for: (list everything from above and anything else on your heart).

I choose to forgive myself for holding onto anger and unforgiveness. I bind and renounce anger and unforgiveness toward (your wife's name). I command anger and unforgiveness toward (your wife's name) to leave me now, in Jesus' name. I command anger and unforgiveness toward (wife's name) to get out and go to the feet of Jesus now. (Breathe deep and believe in faith that these spirits are leaving on your natural exhale.) Father, fill me with Your Spirit. In Jesus' name, amen."

Husbands, forgive me, but I must challenge you even further. The Lord really wants us to clean house.

Husbands are called to love their wives like Christ loved the church.[30] Here's something I came across on Facebook from *Established Family*. Read through it and put a tick beside anything you need to repent for.

"God was willing to lower Himself in human form and die for His Bride. Meanwhile, for our brides... we struggle to make it from Sunday to Sunday without:
>
> Lashing out at them.
> Ignoring their needs.
> Abandoning them emotionally.
> Failing to pursue them with love.
> Withholding spiritual leadership.
> Surrendering our roles as leaders.
> Placing blame instead of protection.
> Choosing comfort over accountability.
> Allowing distractions to steal our focus.
> Seeking validation outside the marriage.
> Neglecting time in prayer for our families.
> Speaking harshly instead of with gentleness.
>
> Being passive in moments that call for action."

Does anything from that list resonate with you? If so, repent below.

Prayer

"Father, I confess that I have (confess all that apply):

- Ignored (wife's name) and my children's needs.
- Abandoned (wife's name) and my children emotionally.
- Failed to pursue (wife's name) with love.
- Withheld spiritual leadership from my family.
- Surrendered my role as a leader in my family.
- Blamed (wife's name) instead of protecting her.
- Chosen comfort over accountability.

- Allowed distractions to steal my focus.
- Sought validation outside of my marriage.
- Neglected time of prayer for my family.
- Spoken harshly instead of with gentleness.
- Been passive in moments when I should have acted.
- Not fulfilled my responsibilities in my marriage and/or home.
- Not defended (wife's name) when I should have.
- Spoken about (wife's name) unbecomingly with others.
- Complained about (wife's name) to others.
- Walked in agreement with fear and shame.

I repent. Please forgive me. I choose to forgive myself and I accept Your forgiveness according to 1 John 1:9. I thank You, God, that I am forgiven. Heal the wounds in my heart that have caused me to behave in these ways.

I repent on behalf of my ancestors and family line, for being harsh and critical toward the boys in the family, for depriving them of their masculine role, putting fear and shame on them, and not allowing them to be boys, for emasculating them and stripping away their courage and strength through humiliation, embarrassment, comparison, belittling, and abuse. Please forgive us. According to 1 John 1:9, I receive Your forgiveness, Lord, on behalf of my ancestors. I choose to forgive my ancestors for behaving in these ways. (If you feel someone has treated you this way, forgive them here.) Lord, I choose to forgive ...... for criticizing, abusing, belittling, and emasculating me; for yelling at me, embarrassing me in front of others and comparing me to others. Father, heal the wounds in my heart that were created by this treatment. Thank You. I receive Your care and healing balm right now. I ask You God to restore my dignity and confidence in who You have made me.

Lord, I ask You to cleanse my bloodline, up and down, from these harmful and diabolical actions toward the boys in the family. With the blood of Jesus, I cut this demonic schematic off of my bloodline right now and I forbid it to continue, in Jesus' name. It stops with me! I declare that my home, my family, my wife, children, and pets are covered in the blood of Jesus and are safe from any demonic transference, in Jesus' name.

I bind and renounce fear, shame, emasculation, abuse, irresponsibility, cowardice, passivity, and apathy in Jesus' name, and I command them to leave me now! Go! Go to the feet of Jesus where you belong and never come back. (Breathe deep and continue to command them to go until you sense relief.) Father, fill me afresh with Your Spirit. Fill me completely full. Don't leave any place in this dwelling empty but fill me completely. In Jesus' name, Amen."

Wonderful! Way to go. I pray you have had a heart-to-heart conversation with your wife as well and chosen to say, "I'm sorry," in addition to renewing your commitment to fulfill your godly role within your family.

You have been set on the right track within your home and family, but you also have a purpose in the Kingdom of God. You were created on purpose with a purpose for Him, so I encourage you to diligently seek the Lord for His direction in your life. Are you working where God wants you to work? Are you following God's call on your life? If you're not fulfilling your godly purpose, your home will be out of order, and this can result in your children being out of order. If you sense a tug on your heart in a change of direction, with godly wisdom, take a step in that direction and see what happens. Most importantly, pray! Seek the Lord for what He would have you do. Strap on your courage and your faith! He is equipping you to be more than you ever expected.

The Resolution for Women

Ladies, you're not getting off scot-free. Sorry. You also have godly roles and responsibilities which you need to fill in the power and enabling of the Holy Spirit. I'm sure there are things that you will need to repent for, and you will need to forgive your husband for how you feel he has failed you and your children.

First off, let's tackle the anger and unforgiveness in your heart toward your husband and then forgive him for how he has not shown up for you.

Prayer

"Father, I confess that I have been harboring anger and unforgiveness in my heart toward (husband's name). I repent. Please forgive me. I choose to forgive (husband's name) for (check those that apply and add your own):

- Not loving me in the way I can receive.
- Not spending more time with me.
- Not taking me out on dates.
- Not completing the tasks around the house that need to be done, in a timely manner.
- Lashing out at me and the children in frustration and/or anger.
- Ignoring my needs and the needs of our children.
- Abandoning us emotionally.
- Failing to pursue me with love.
- Withholding spiritual leadership from our family.
- Surrendering his role as the leader in our home.
- Blaming me instead of protecting me.
- Choosing his comfort over accountability.
- Allowing distractions to steal his focus.
- Seeking validation outside our marriage.
- Neglecting time in prayer for our family.
- Speaking harshly instead of with gentleness.
- Being passive in moments that call for action.
- Not defending me.
- Speaking about me negatively.

Father, heal every wound in my heart created by his sinful actions. And forgive me God, for not responding to (husband's name) in a loving way. Thank You for Your forgiveness. I bind and renounce anger and unforgiveness toward (husband's name) and I command them to leave me now, in Jesus' name. Go! Go to the feet of Jesus and never come back. (Breathe and believe in faith that these spirits are leaving on your natural breath.)

Lord, fill me up with Your Spirit to overflowing, Amen."

Okay, let's look at *The Resolution for Women* from the book with the same name by Priscilla Shirer. It goes as follows:

"I WILL embrace my current season of life and live with a spirit of gratitude and contentment.

I WILL champion God's model for womanhood and teach it to my children.

I WILL celebrate my God-given uniqueness and the distinctions He has placed on others.

I WILL live as a woman answerable to God and faithfully committed to His Word.

I WILL seek to devote the best of myself to the primary roles God has entrusted to me.

I WILL be quick to listen, slow to speak, and esteem others more highly than myself.

I WILL forgive those who have wronged me and reconcile with those I have wronged.

I WILL not tolerate evil influences in myself or my home but will embrace a life of purity.

I WILL pursue justice, love mercy, and extend compassion toward others.

I WILL be faithful to my husband and honor him in my conduct and in my conversation, and will aspire to be a suitable partner for him to help him reach his God-given potential.

> I WILL teach my children to love God, respect authority, and live responsibly.
>
> I WILL cultivate a peaceful and grace-filled life where God's presence is sensed.
>
> I WILL make today's decisions with tomorrow's impact in mind and consider my current choices in light of future generations.
>
> I WILL courageously work with the strength God provides to fulfill this resolution for the rest of my life and for His glory.
>
> As for me and my house, we will serve the Lord (Joshua 24:15 NASB)."[31]

I would encourage you to read through that resolution slowly and thoughtfully. And as you do, ask the Holy Spirit to show you how you have fallen short.

When I first began looking at this resolution and reading the book, the very first chapter which addresses the first point in the resolution, sucker punched me in the gut. "I WILL embrace my current season of life and live with a spirit of gratitude and contentment." The words that grabbed me the most are: embrace, current, and contentment. To be content in and with our current season in every season, no matter how difficult, challenges me personally but I also feel it doesn't apply to all situations. There are times when we must rise and say, "Nope, this is not God's best for me. Something is out of order and the enemy is taking advantage of it," and then do what is necessary to close the access points that the devil may be using to cause havoc in our lives. I would never expect anyone going through a really difficult time to just be content with it.

Priscilla's point was to not miss the current season by always looking ahead to the next—to be 100% present in the present and embrace it. I get that. But for our purposes in this book, I don't think we should ever be content in circumstances that are clearly not godly. That is not to say we should try to control other people and what they do, but to always take stock of ourselves and allow God to correct us when needed.

What we *can* be content in, is knowing that God is for us and is working with us to bring healing and restoration to our children and families. We *can* be grateful and content in the truth that we will not and do not have to live in chaos because Jesus is a God of order, love, and peace and Jesus is King over our home. He has ALL authority there because we give Him ALL authority there.

So, other than not being content with your current situation of misbehaving children, is the Holy Spirit convicting you of anything else? Perhaps there are other things in your life that the Holy Spirit is challenging you to be content with. Your living arrangements perhaps? Your home? Your husband? Your bank account? Your job? Yourself? Is the Lord calling you to be content with who you are? To give yourself grace?

Contentment is birthed out of gratitude. When we are sincerely grateful for who we are and what we have, we become content; we are then positioned with the Lord in such a way that His hand can be released to bless us even more.

Remember the Israelites in the desert? Remember how much they complained against God for what they didn't have? God caused Manna to rain down from the sky every day so they would have food to eat, yet they complained about not having the foods they were used to enjoying back in Egypt like fish, cucumbers, melons, leeks, onions, and garlic. If I'm honest, I probably would have complained too. (Eating the same thing every day for forty years is not MY idea of fun.) Something in one season may not *feel* like God's best, but if we're not grateful for what He gives us, we probably won't see increase until we are.

Are you walking in discontentment? What is the fruit of discontentment? If we are discontent, we will be driven to find contentment, somewhere, somehow, and that may materialize in needless overspending, or a constant searching for the next best thing to be a part of whether it's an extracurricular activity, class, friendship, or volunteer opportunity. We will always be searching for what will satisfy and make us happy.

Let's pray for a release from discontentment, dissatisfaction, entitlement, and ungratefulness. Please just skip over whatever does not apply to you.

Prayer

"Father, forgive me for walking in agreement with discontentment, dissatisfaction, entitlement, and ungratefulness. I repent.

I confess that I've been angry at You God for not providing more for our family. I repent. Please forgive me.

I confess that I have been angry at (husband's name) for not bringing more resources into our home and not getting a better paying job. I repent. Please forgive me.

I choose to forgive You, God. I choose to forgive (husband's name). And I choose to forgive myself for not being grateful, for not having a correct perspective of You, God and for not being content with what I have. I receive Your forgiveness, Lord, according to 1 John 1:9 and I declare that I am forgiven by the blood of Your Son, Jesus. Lord, heal every wound in my heart that caused me to operate in these things.

I choose to come out of these destructive attitudes right now. I renounce and divorce myself from discontentment, dissatisfaction, entitlement, and ungratefulness and I command these things to loose me now, in Jesus' name. Discontentment, dissatisfaction, entitlement, and ungratefulness, leave me now and go to the feet of Jesus where you belong! (Breathe deep and blow these things out of your mouth in faith.) Holy Spirit, fill me up with Your abiding presence. Don't leave any place in my body or soul untouched by You.

Thank You, Lord, for Who You are on my behalf. Thank You for all You provide for us. And thank You for (husband's name) and how hard he works. Bless him, God, with Your peace and strength to continue walking with You and doing his best for us. In Jesus' name, amen."

Beautiful.

If you have dishonored or disrespected your husband in any way, please pray the following:

Prayer

> "Father, forgive me for walking in agreement with dishonor and disrespect toward (husband's name). I repent."

If you have cursed your husband with unkind words or name-calling, renounce your words here.

> "I repent for saying that (husband's name) is..... and I renounce my words, in Jesus' name. Please forgive me, God, for speaking what You are NOT speaking about (husband's name). I command my negative words to fall to the ground now, in Jesus' name and I break every curse empowered by them, with the blood of Jesus."

If you feel you need to forgive your husband for anything that may have triggered your disrespect, please do that here.

> "I choose to forgive (husband's name) for.....
>
> I choose to forgive myself and I receive Your forgiveness, Lord. Heal every wound in my heart that caused me to speak and behave in ungodly ways toward (husband's name).
>
> I bind, renounce and divorce myself from dishonor and disrespect toward my husband and I command them to leave me now, in Jesus' name. Dishonor and disrespect, go to the feet of Jesus where you belong. (Breathe deep and blow them out in faith. Continue to command them to go until you sense a

release.) Holy Spirit, fill me afresh with Your presence, completely full, in Jesus' name. Amen"

If there is anything else the Holy Spirit has convicted you of my sister, please pray through it now.

This concludes our time of reconciliation between husbands and wives. I pray you have been able to work through your wounds together and forgive one another so you can stand united against the schemes of the devil in your home.

Let's continue.

ELIMINATING FEAR

Fear is such a prevalent issue; it needs a chapter all its own and we need to kick it ALL in the butt and out in Jesus' name.

The spirit or demon of fear is a strongman spirit, which means it is a ruling spirit and has other smaller spirits under it working on its behalf. "What other spirits?" you might ask. Well, spirits of the fear of certain things, like any of the following:

- Fear of heights
- Fear of tight spaces
- Fear of spiders
- Fear of the dark
- Fear of rejection
- Fear of abandonment
- Fear of not being loved

- Fear of failure
- Fear of anything

Now, if any of those apply to you or your children, you will need to pray through them, however, in this chapter I want to focus on fears that we as parents might have regarding our children because any and every fear is an open door to the enemy to harass us and our family. We all know that fear is not of God. (The *fear of God* is a whole other thing; this is recognizing the power and supremacy of God and being in awe of Him.) Second Timothy 1:7 says, "For God has not given us a spirit of fear, but of power and of love and of a sound mind" (NKJV). So, if God did not give us a spirit of fear, the devil must have given it to us (and we cooperated with him by receiving it).

There are three specific fears that the Lord is impressing upon me to discuss. They are the following: the spirit of the fear of poverty, the spirit of the fear of our children being homosexual, and the spirit of the fear of our kids' complete mental health breakdown and/or committing suicide. (I am truly, truly, sorry if you have already experienced this tragedy in your family. My heart breaks for all involved. Please accept my sincere condolences.)

Fear of Poverty

I don't think I need to explain too much here. I have a feeling a lot of readers know exactly what this is and also know it is operating in them.

Are you afraid of not having enough in the future? Are you afraid of losing your job or not having an income to pay the bills? Are you afraid of losing your house? Are you afraid of not being able to provide for your kiddos? Are you afraid of not having enough money to pay for upcoming expenses like college? Are you afraid of your credit card bill? Do you get a sick feeling in your gut when you're constantly having to buy things or pay bills? Just last week I stood at the counter in our local vet's office paying an $800 emergency bill for our cat and felt light-headed, like I might pass out. Hello? This is the fear of poverty!

It is truly mind boggling the expenses we incur *and allow* in our lives to maintain our standard of living in North America and the things we want. Let's be real friends. I don't need to have three cats in my home along with all the expenses they incur, but for some reason I feel responsible for every stray cat at my door. I need healing! And I am getting it from my beautiful, faithful Father. Praise God.

What about you? Do you incur unnecessary expenses due to skewed responsibilities or desires? If so, ask Pappa God what the root of that is and He will show you when you're ready to receive it.

We as North Americans truly are spoiled. Our way of life is seeped in entitlement, comfort, and excess and our culture is saturated with a Babylonian (or worldly) demon of consumerism. It compels us to consume and spend! Consume and spend. Have you ever been on a mission trip to an impoverished place? If not, you should go. You will get an attitude adjustment real fast. Nothing else will adjust your perspective and make you realize all the unnecessary things you have than that.

I remember coming back from Mexico and Bolivia having an overwhelming need to give away half of my closet when we returned. I realized just how ridiculous and excessive it was for me to have so much when others had hardly anything. Short-term missions removes the veil of familiar Babylon from our vision and helps us see truth and reality better. No one can feel good about having thirty pairs of shoes when a little child living in a dirty cardboard shelter has none. It's impossible, if you have the Spirit of Jesus living in your heart.

I will always advocate to parents, "Take your child (children) on short-term missions and let them see how other people in the world live. Get them out of their little bubble and into reality. I would be willing to bet that suddenly they become much more appreciative of what they have and a whole lot more empathetic toward others."

Here's the issue with the fear of poverty. It puts us into hoarding mode. It makes us collect stuff we don't need and save things we will never use. It makes us takers, not givers and here's what 2 Corinthians 9:6-8 says about that:

> Remember this: Whoever sows sparingly will also reap sparingly, and whoever sows generously will also reap generously. Each of you should give what you have decided in your heart to give, not reluctantly or under compulsion, for God loves a cheerful giver. And God is able to bless you abundantly, so that in all things at all times, having all that you need, you will abound in every good work" (NIV).

If we sow generously, we will reap generously, but our hearts need to be clear of the fear of poverty before we will *want* to be givers according to God's desire. The *wanting* part is key! God does not want us to give if we feel pressured to give or obligated to give. We must give when we have it in our hearts to do so. "Father, cause us to want what You want."

I would encourage you, before you pray the prayer below, to contemplate with the Lord where this fear came from. I would suggest it is rooted in something that happened or something you witnessed as a child. Perhaps you saw your parents struggling financially. Perhaps you heard their concerns about money. Perhaps they said to you, "We can't afford that," or they communicated to you somehow that you were a burden to them financially. Perhaps your family was evicted from housing for not being able to pay the rent. Perhaps your mom had to sell your favorite toy in order to pay rent. Perhaps you watched your schoolmates enjoy a nice lunch from a fancy X-men or Barbie box while you had nothing. Perhaps you had to wear the same pair of worn-out shoes every day while other kids had new shoes every six months. Perhaps your parent instilled fear in you by saying things like, "You better go to college so you can get a good paying job. Everything is getting more and more expensive! You're not going to be able to support a family with that job. You're never going to be able to buy a house." We all know, as parents, that life and finances are stressful. And it is so easy to speak things out without really considering their affect on a child's psyche.

What was it in your childhood that made you fear poverty or expect poverty in your own life? Perhaps you just accepted the lie that it was normal to live in lack. You do business with God. Let Him show you and then tell Him back how you felt as a child about money and provision. How did your parents make you feel about this subject? Journal about it. There may be a few different things that created the stronghold in your mind to fear poverty. Make sure you forgive every person in every instance who set you up to live in this lie. Repent for believing lies and forgive yourself for believing lies, then replace the lies with the truth of God's Word.

Okay, when you're ready, let's get rid of the fear of poverty.

Prayer

"Heavenly Father, we love You and we thank You for Who You are. Surround me/us with Your delivering power now. I/we confess that I/we have agreed with the fear of poverty. I/we have been afraid of not having enough, losing my/our source of income... etc. (list any fears related to poverty and finances). I/we have not trusted You to be nor looked to You to be our Provider. I/we have been working to obtain what I/we already have in You—complete security, safety, and abundance in all things. I/we repent. Please forgive me/us. I/We choose to forgive myself/ourselves and I/we receive Your forgiveness according to 1 John 1:9 and release myself/ourselves from all guilt, condemnation, and unrighteousness. I/We am/are forgiven and washed in Your blood. In the authority You have given me/us, I/we bind the spirit of fear right now in Jesus' name and I/we resist its maneuvers against me/us. I/we renounce the fear of poverty in Jesus' name, and I/we command it to leave me/us now. You will come up and out and go to the feet of Jesus and not return. I/we am/are done with you! Get out now, in Jesus' name. (Breathe deep and in faith believe that the spirit is leaving your body on your natural breathing.) Father, fill me/us with Your Holy Spirit and occupy every place in me/us that has been vacated. I/we want to be saturated in You! In Jesus' name, amen."

Fear of Homosexuality in Your Children

This fear may be less common, however, may be on the rise with the LGBTQ community so prevalent and loud in our schools, infiltrating curriculum and school reading materials. Specifically, I am referring to the fear that your children will turn out to be gay.

First, I want to clarify my beliefs (which I believe to be godly and come from the Holy Spirit) around what makes someone homosexual. I believe there is a demonic spirit of homosexuality that has attached to those who are gay through a spiritual open door in their life which could be any of the following:

- Homosexual behavior in previous generations.
- In the case a gay boy, deep father wounds (ie. not having their biological father in their life or having one that was detached and emotionally unavailable).
- In the case of a lesbian, deep mother wounds (ie. not having their biological mother in their life or having one that was detached and emotionally unavailable).
- Rejection or perceived rejection from their biological father or mother.
- Experimenting with homosexual behavior.
- Viewing homosexual pornography.
- Sexual abuse/molestation inflicted by someone of the same sex.

- A girl sexually abused by a man rejecting men, as an adult, because she sees them as unsafe.
- Adolescents giving into curiosity and experimenting with sexual activity with someone of the same sex.
- Deep shame and hopelessness.

This homosexual spirit distorts the perception of a person causing them to be attracted to the same gender.

When does this happen? It can vary. But it *can* attach itself to a baby *in utero* causing a child to be born gay. In such case, it can happen because of generational iniquity, having a gay mother, (in the case of a boy) having a biological father who rejects him, or (in the case of a girl) having a biological mother who rejects her. In this last scenario, I believe the demon *can* attach to the baby before birth depending on the opportunity for the enemy in the mother OR attach to the baby after birth.

It is an emotional need in all of us to attach emotionally to our mother and father. If a baby girl is rejected by her mother, she will have a continuous void in her heart which she may eventually attempt to fill with the validation from another female. She *may*, without any intervention from the Lord, form a soul tie with another girl out of her desperation to be accepted by another female who represents to her a mother figure. The corresponding scenario could happen for a baby boy who is rejected by his father.

Please note, I am NOT saying that *every* girl who has been rejected by her mother will be gay nor will every boy who has been rejected by his father be gay; there are many other factors to consider, but they will both have a void in their heart. If that void is not filled with someone godly (like an aunt, uncle, adoptive parent etc.) they may turn to friendships which *may* in turn become twisted. The enemy is very crafty at filling the minds of young people with lies about their worth and their identity, especially if they've been rejected.

I share all of this with you to hopefully give you some understanding of how someone becomes gay. It is not something that God does. He does not create gay people. It is not His design; it is a perversion of our perception from the enemy. Remember that as soon as a child is conceived, they are alive and enter this world. They are unseen and hidden in the womb, covered by muscle, tissue, and skin, but they are very much alive and in the world with all of its chaos and fallen attributes. When a baby is conceived it is *immediately* subject to the spiritual warfare that rages all around us, in the womb and out.

Okay, so let's focus back on the fear of having a gay child. When did you first think that it was a possibility for your child to be gay? What was happening that made you think that?

For example, if we were programmed (as a child) to believe that girls play with dolls and boys play with trucks, as soon as we see that our girl wants to play with trucks and our boy wants to play with dolls, the enemy takes advantage of that opportunity and plants the thought in our mind, "Oh no. Maybe my son/daughter is gay." Let me be clear. This is a lie from the devil! No child is ever created gay. Unfortunately, though, as soon we entertain the fear that our child might be gay and believe that lie, we've opened a door through which the enemy can access our child. Unfortunately, because of that, we may one day see our fear realized. So, let's pray and kick this fear out.

Prayer

"Heavenly Father, we love You and we thank You for Who You are. Surround me/us with Your delivering power now. I/we confess that I/we have agreed with the fear of homosexuality for our children. I/we have been afraid of my/our child (children) being gay (list any other fears related to their sexuality). I/we have not trusted You to protect my/our child/children nor be his/her/their wonderful Creator Who only creates children made in Your image. I/we repent. Please forgive me/us. I/We choose to forgive myself/ourselves and I/we receive Your forgiveness according to 1 John 1:9 and release myself/ourselves from all guilt, condemnation, and unrighteousness. I/We am/are forgiven and washed in Your blood. In the authority You have given me/us, I/we bind the spirit of fear right now in Jesus' name and I/we resist its maneuvers against me/us. I/we renounce the fear of homosexuality and perversion in Jesus' name, and I/we command it to leave me/us now. You will come up and out and go to the feet of Jesus and not return. I/we am/are done with you! Get out now, in Jesus' name. (Breathe deep and in faith believe that the spirit is leaving your body on your natural breathing.) Father, we choose to believe that You are a good, good Father Who can be trusted with everything, even our children. Father, fill me/us with Your Holy Spirit and occupy every place in me/us that has been vacated. I/we want to be saturated in You! Amen."

Good work my friend. You have dealt with the fear in your heart, and we will deal with the spirit of homosexuality that may be on your kids in the last chapter of the book when we get into the warfare on their behalf. For now, let's move on to the fear of mental illness and suicide.

Fear of Suicide

Beloved, we must surrender our children to God. He is their best Father, and they actually need Him more than they need us. We are flawed, but God is not. He knows how to love them perfectly.

First, I suggest you ask the Holy Spirit if there is something in your past that makes you susceptible to this fear. Was there anyone else in your family who was at risk for, attempted or committed suicide? Was there another time when you partnered with this fear? If so, you will need to ask the Lord to heal the wounds in your heart and forgive the people involved.

Additionally, was there anyone around you that suggested to you (put the suggestion in your mind) that suicide was a risk factor for your child/children? Was there legitimacy to that suggestion at the time? One of two things could have happened. First, if it was a legitimate concern at the time, it could have been God alerting you to pray and break it. Second, if it wasn't a legitimate concern at the time, it could have been the enemy using that person to plant the suggestion and fear in your mind. In this case, I would pray, "I reject their suggestion, and I break the power of their words over *(say child's name)* in Jesus' name. And I choose to forgive them for putting a voice to it." Then continue to pray the prayer coming up.

If *you* have seen or witnessed something in your child's behavior that has sparked a thought or concern about their mental health to the extent that you think they may commit suicide, do not give in to fear and do not believe the lie. Rather pray for them IN FAITH. In faith, is the key. All too often, we pray out of fear and this type of praying is ineffective. The Lord sees your heart and is compassionate toward you, but the scriptures say, "...without faith it is impossible to please God..." (Hebrews 11:6a NIV). Without faith, your prayers don't move anyone. They don't move the hand of God, they don't stay the hand of the enemy, and they don't move angels to work on your behalf.

How do we pray in faith in this regard? Like this:

Prayer

"I/we thank You, God, for *(say child's name)*. I/we thank You that she/he is in Your hands, and no one can remove her/him from them. (skip the next part if it doesn't apply to you and continue below.)

> (If you've had someone in your family commit suicide or attempt to commit suicide, pray: "Lord, as You know, (person's name) attempted (or committed) suicide and I was greatly wounded and traumatized by it. (Give God more detail if it's heavy on your heart.) Lord, I ask You to heal me of all trauma related to it and heal every wound in my heart created by it. Lord, I confess that I have held onto anger and unforgiveness in my heart

toward (person's name) for a long time. I repent and I ask You to forgive me. I renounce anger and I renounce unforgiveness, in Jesus' name and I command both to leave me now. You will come up and out and go to the feet of Jesus and not return. (Breathe deep and trust that the spirits are leaving on your natural breathing). I choose right now to forgive (name of person) for attempting (or committing) suicide and traumatizing me and my family. I renounce trauma and I command it to leave me now, in Jesus' name. Trauma you will come up and out and go to the feet of Jesus right now. Go! And never come back. (Breathe deep and trust that trauma is leaving on your natural breathing.))

Continue...

I/we confess, Lord, that I/we have been in the fear of (say child's name) having mental illness and committing suicide. I/we repent. Please forgive me/us. I/we choose to forgive myself/ourselves and I/we declare that I/we am/are forgiven and cleansed from the fear of mental illness and suicide relating to my/our children. I/we bind the spirit of fear, and I/we renounce the fear of my child(ren) committing suicide. I/we command it to leave me/us now, in Jesus' name. Fear of suicide, you will come up and out and go to the feet of Jesus, right now! Never to return. (Breathe deep and in faith believe that it is leaving you on your natural breathing.) Lord, fill me/us up with Your Spirit and don't leave any place untouched by Your power and love. Thank You, Father. I/we receive You now, in Jesus' name. Empower me/us, God, to walk in faith and not fear.

And now, I/we stand in the authority that You, God, have given me/us as Your family and representatives on the earth, and we come to You on behalf of *(say child's name)*, our daughter/son. We ask You, God, to forgive her/him for entertaining thoughts and lies about her/his worth and possibly about suicide. Forgive her, God, for partnering with fear, heaviness, depression, suicide, and lies. We plead for Your mercy, God, over her/his life. Thank You, Lord, that You are close to the broken-hearted. Pour out Your love and truth into her/his heart and cause Your Spirit to hover over her/him. Open the window of heaven around her and over her, so she/he can hear Your voice.

And in the authority You have given me/us according to Luke 10:19, I/we cancel every assignment and scheme of the enemy over *(say child's name)*. I/we arrest each and every lie that Satan has whispered into *(say child's name)*'s heart and mind and in the power of Yeshua, I/we tear them down with force. I/we cancel and reverse every negative thought and word, in Jesus' name. I/we renounce the lie that we would be better off without her/him, and I/we break its power in *(say child's name)*'s life. I/we renounce the lie that *(say child's name)* is susceptible to mental illness, depression, suicide, and (any other mental illness that you have been afraid of her/him suffering from; perhaps some sort of condition that has run in your family). The blood of Jesus is enough for her/him, and it works on her/his behalf, protecting her/him and creating a barrier of fire and power to resist the enemy. I/we declare that every generational curse related to mental illness is broken now. Jesus hung on a cross and became a curse for us so curses would no longer operate in our lives. He finished the work on our behalf, overcoming the enemy and destroying all his works. The devil has no more authority to cause us harm; he has been disarmed and is now the "forever loser."

Greater are You, God, Who is in *(say child's name)* than he that is in the world. I/we declare that the voice of God in *(say child's name)*'s spirit will be louder than any voice of the enemy. I/we put a gag order on the enemy right now in Jesus' name and plead the blood of Jesus over *(say child's name)*'s mind. I/we bind every spirit of depression, heaviness, and suicide attached to (child's mind). I/we tie them up with chains right now, resist their maneuvers, break their illegitimate, illegal, use of power and command them to leave *(say child's name)* now, right where she/he is. I/we command them to leave her/him now upon her/his natural breathing. Heaviness, depression and suicide, I/we send you to the feet of Jesus right now. Come up and out now upon *(say child's name)*'s natural breathing. I/we forbid you to cause her/him any harm or grief, in Jesus' name. I/we declare complete freedom for *(say child's name)* from all depression, heaviness, and suicide in the mighty name of Jesus. Father, we ask You to fill *(say child's name)* with Your Spirit afresh and completely. In Jesus' name, amen."

STANDING FOR YOUR FAMILY

KINGS AND PRIESTS

> For those God foreknew he also predestined to be conformed to the image of his Son, that he might be the firstborn among many brothers and sisters (Romans 8:29 NIV).

Jesus Christ is the King of kings and is our High Priest interceding for us at the right hand of God.[32] Hebrews 4:14 says, "Seeing then that we have a great High Priest who has passed through the heavens, Jesus the Son of God, let us hold fast our confession" (NKJV). Jesus is the One Who represents us to the Father.

Jesus is also the King of kings, the One Who represents God to us and the world. He rules His Kingdom and just as Jesus was commissioned by God, His Father, we are commissioned by Jesus to rule our house in His ways, in His power (not our own strength). Jesus said in John 20:21, "So

Jesus said to them again, "Peace unto you! As the Father has sent Me, I also send you" (NKJV). And just as Romans 8:29 says, we have been predestined to be changed into the image of Jesus, we can conclude that . . .

WE ARE CALLED BY GOD TO BE KINGS AND PRIESTS IN OUR OWN HOME UNDER THE HEADSHIP OF CHRIST.

Just as Jesus fulfilled two roles . . . King and Priest, we are to as well.

What does this mean? A king rules the kingdom, and a king also represents God to the people of the kingdom. What is *our* kingdom? Our kingdom is our home and our sphere of influence. In conclusion, we are to represent God to our children, govern our home in a godly way and bring the presence of God into our home through praise, worship, and thanksgiving. We are to model to our children what Jesus looks like and create an atmosphere of Him where we live.

Being a priest in our home means we represent our children before God; we bring their sin before Him and pray for mercy and grace in their lives. We go up in intercession and we come down full of godly wisdom and direction to govern our family's spiritual condition and the atmosphere of our home.

As I was preparing to write this chapter, the Lord prompted me to read through 1 Kings and part of 2 Kings. All I can say is, "What a fiasco!" It's so disheartening how Israel and Judah rebelled against God by worshipping the false gods of other nations, but the following is the Lord's purpose: to open our eyes to what rebellion against Him looks like and to allow His Word to read us.

We know that King David was a man after God's own heart and David's son, Solomon, did exceedingly well as king until he grew old. His downfall? Women. 1 Kings 11:1-6 says:

> King Solomon, however, loved many foreign women besides Pharaoh's daughter—Moabites, Ammonites, Edomites, Sidonians, and Hittites. They were from nations about which the LORD had told the Israelites, "You must not intermarry with them, because they will surely turn your hearts after their gods." Nevertheless, Solomon held fast to them in love. He had seven hundred wives of royal birth and three hundred concubines, and his wives led him astray. As Solomon grew old, his wives turned his heart after other gods, and his heart was not fully devoted to the LORD his God, as the heart of David his father had been. He followed Ashtoreth the goddess of the Sidonians, and Molek the detestable god of the Ammonites. So Solomon did evil in the eyes of the LORD; he did not follow the LORD completely, as David his father had done" (NIV).

After Solomon's death, the northern tribes of Israel rebelled against the south, and Israel was divided into two nations: Israel and Judah (The House of David). Idolatry, then continued being passed down through the generations of Israel's and Judah's kings. There were a few faithful kings here and there in Jerusalem (southern/Judah), but each time, the very *next* king ruined it for them all by doing evil in the eyes of the Lord, again.

Finally, God had enough. In 722 BC, the northern kingdom, Israel, was overtaken by the king of Assyria; he captured Samaria and deported the Israelites to Assyria (2 Kings 17:6). And in 597 BC, the Babylonians completed their occupation of Jerusalem by destroying it and carrying off into exile all who remained in the city, except for the poorest of the poor who stayed back to work the fields and vineyards (2 Kings 25:8-12). Here's a detailed account of what they did:

> ⁷All this took place because the Israelites had sinned against the LORD their God, who had brought them up out of Egypt from under the power of Pharaoh king of Egypt. They worshipped other gods ⁸and followed the practices of the nations the LORD had driven out before them, as well as the practices that the kings of Israel had introduced. ⁹The Israelites secretly did things against the LORD their God that were not right. From watchtower to fortified city they built themselves high places in all their towns. ¹⁰They set up sacred stones and Asherah poles on every high hill and under every spreading tree. ¹¹At every high place they burned incense, as the nations whom the LORD had driven out before them had done. They did wicked things that aroused the LORD'S anger. ¹²They worshipped idols, though the LORD had said, "You shall not do this." ¹³The LORD warned Israel and Judah through all his prophets and seers: "Turn from your evil ways. Observe my commands and decrees, in accordance with the entire Law that I commanded your ancestors to obey and that I delivered to you through my servants the

prophets." ¹⁴But they would not listen and were as stiff-necked as their ancestors, who did not trust in the LORD their God. ¹⁵They rejected his decrees and the covenant he had made with their ancestors and the statutes he had warned them to keep. They followed worthless idols and themselves became worthless. They imitated the nations around them although the LORD had ordered them, "Do not do as they do." ¹⁶They forsook all the commands of the LORD their God and made for themselves two idols cast in the shape of calves, and an Asherah pole. They bowed down to all the starry hosts, and they worshipped Baal. ¹⁷They sacrificed their sons and daughters in the fire. They practiced divination and sought omens and sold themselves to do evil in the eyes of the LORD, arousing his anger. ¹⁸So the LORD was very angry with Israel and removed them from his presence. Only the tribe of Judah was left, ¹⁹and even Judah did not keep the commands of the LORD their God. They followed the practices Israel had introduced. ²⁰Therefore the LORD rejected all the people of Israel; he afflicted them and gave them into the hands of plunderers, until he thrust them from his presence" (2 Kings 17:7-20 NIV).

From the kings of Israel and Judah we learn that idolatry is taken very seriously by the Lord. We also know from the example of Eli and his sons that as a priest in our home, we must fulfill our role appropriately by holding our children accountable and teaching them to walk in holiness, as well as how to repent when they miss the mark. (Eli was held accountable by the Lord for not restraining his sons from their sin (see 1 Sam. 2:30-36 & 1 Sam. 3:12-14 & 1 Sam. 4:10-11).) Both roles, king and priest, require committed and complete surrender and devotion to God.

We are under a better covenant now, yes, and we can find forgiveness when we confess our sins, but we must never take mercy or grace for granted. Grace is not a licence to sin but an empowerment, through the Holy Spirit, NOT to sin. We must always be living a life of repentance.

So, friends, how has the Word read you through this chapter? Have you allowed the Holy Spirit to convict you where you need to be convicted? We must seek the Lord for revelation on how we are cooperating with idolatry in our own lives and the lives of our children. We may not be fashioning golden calves but there are certainly many ways we can devote ourselves to and rely on things that bring us comfort, or entertainment, or help us relax or give us some sense of control over what may feel like a very stressful existence. Idolatry doesn't have to look like it did in the Old Testament; it can look like loving, or enjoying, or relying on someone else or something else as much or more than God.

What do you turn to when you're stressed? Would you be able to stop turning to that thing if the Lord asked you to?

What do you turn to when you need comfort?

What has made you the most disappointed? Why are you so disappointed about that? Why was it so important to you?

What do you complain about and why? Is there an idol there?

What makes you unreasonably mad? Is there an idol there?

Is there anything that you would not be willing to give up if the Lord asked you to?

Who or what is sitting on the throne of your heart?

Whose encouragement or approval means the most to you? Are they on the throne of your heart?

Who have you expected to make you happy? Should they have that much power of you?

All these questions can help us identify idols in our life.

God is not willing to share the throne of your heart with anyone or anything else.

Finaly, what have you allowed in your home that has caused your children to fall into idolatry? How have you failed to be a godly king in your home, leading your children to worship only the One true God, Jehovah? How have you failed to lead your children in their spiritual journey? Many times, we want to abdicate that responsibility to the church, but God holds us, the parents, responsible for it.

Proverbs 22:6 says, "Train up a child in the way he should go, And when he is old he will not depart from it" (NKJV). Deuteronomy 11:18-21 says:

> Fix these words of mine in your hearts and minds; tie them as symbols on your hands and bind them on your foreheads. Teach them to your children, talking about them when you sit at home and when you walk along the road, when you lie down and when you get up. Write them on the doorframes of your houses and on your gates, so that your days and the days of your children may be many in the land the Lord swore to give your ancestors, as many as the days that the heavens are above the earth" (NIV).

We are not to be bystanders to the teaching and spiritual training of our children. It is first and foremost our job, given to us by the Lord.

When you think about it, Sunday School or Children's Church has our children for only 1.5 hours, give or take, per week. If your children go to mid-week programs, perhaps it's 3 or 4 hours per week. That's being generous. The school your children attend is influencing them for 30 hours per week, assuming they go to school outside of your home. Again, assuming they are not home-schooled, you have approximately 50 hours per week with them at home when they are awake. If you take into consideration time spent cooking meals, doing homework and extra curricular activities, you're down to less than 40, but it's still way more than the time spent at church. You are your children's best and most effective educator and influencer and the one with the greatest opportunity to teach and train them well.

I'd like to suggest you take two steps in this chapter. First, I suggest identifying your idols and secondly, identify the idols in your children's lives. Within each of those steps, I'd like to also suggest two action steps. First, pray to renounce idolatry and break soul ties with the idols and secondly, remove the idols from your home.

Your Idols

Spend some time in prayer and ask the Holy Spirit to show you if you have any idols. Write them down and get ready to pray the prayer coming up to come out of agreement with them.

Now, I'd like you to ask yourself the following: "Did I think that marriage was going to be the answer to all my problems?

Or did you think, before you were married, that your spouse was going to be the answer to all your problems? If so, either your marriage or your spouse is on the throne of your heart, and they/it needs to come down.

As we move into the prayers, please do not think that you can just read them, for them to be effective. You must speak the prayers out loud, with conviction and authority, bringing your heart and faith into agreement with them. If you need to read through them first, do that, then speak them out loud in faith.

Prayers

For general idols:

> "Father, forgive me for walking in agreement with idolatry. Forgive me for idolizing... (name the idol). I confess that it has been too important to me. I repent. I renounce idolatry and I surrender this idol to You, Lord. I give it up. And I break any soul tie that I've had with it—any emotional or physiological dependence I've developed with it, I break it now in Jesus' name. I choose to divorce this idol, and I give it to You; I ask You to take it and destroy it. Lord, I ask You to heal the wounds in my heart that caused me to become attached to it. I renounce the spirit of addiction to... (name the idol) in Jesus' name and I command idolatry and addiction to leave me now! You will come up and out and go to the feet of Jesus right now. (Breathe deep and continue to command it to go until you sense a release.) Father, fill me up with Your Holy

Spirit. Don't leave any place in me not filled with You. In Jesus' name, amen."

If your spouse or marriage has been on the throne of your heart:

"Father, forgive me for placing my spouse, (say his/her name), and/or my marriage, on the throne of my heart. I am sorry that I have expected You to share that throne, only meant for You, with them. I repent. And I remove them from that throne now. I choose to love You, God, first and most and rely on You as my primary source of everything. Lord, heal every wound in my heart that caused me to idolize... ("my marriage" or your spouse's name). I now break every ungodly portion of my soul tie and emotional connection with my spouse and I remove it from myself now. Every demon attached to my spouse that has accessed me through our union, I command it to loose me now in Jesus' name. I renounce idolatry and I command it to go from me now, in Jesus' name. I command it to go to the feet of Jesus. (Breathe deep and continue to command it to go until you sense a release.) I declare the fire of God around me to protect me from any more ungodly transference. Thank You, Lord for Your freedom. Fill me with Your Spirit, in Jesus' name. Amen."

Finally, ask the Holy Spirit what you need to purge from your home that does not glorify Him. Make a list and dispose of the things God shows you.

Your Children's Idols

What is your child or children addicted to? What are they "obsessed" with? What is it they can't go the whole day without doing or watching or playing with? Are they addicted to a game? A certain toy? A certain video, movie or show?

Ask the Holy Spirit to show you everything that is of concern and make a list. Ask the Holy Spirit what it is about the game or show that makes it addictive. Or what is it the child is getting from that toy or activity? (Possibilities are a sense of power, control or justice, emotional comfort, or simply a "rush" of adrenaline.) This will give you, as the parent, an idea of what your child needs. If they are getting a sense of control from what they are playing or watching, ask yourself where they feel out of control in their life and why. To remedy the situation, perhaps you can give them more age-appropriate choices throughout their day, so they feel like they have more control over simple things. (Example: "Would you like to wear this or that today?" Would you like cereal or eggs for breakfast?" "Would you like to wear that coat or this coat?" "Would you like milk or bubbly water to drink?" etc.)

It is vital that parents strap on their godly wisdom in this area and take it seriously. We think that an obsession with a toy is harmless, but it is not, especially if your child is having behavior problems and emotional outbursts of anger. There is something that has captured your child's emotions, intellect, or spirit if they are "obsessed" with anything. "Are they really obsessed with it," you may ask. Well, how do they respond when you take it away? Do they fly into a rage? If so, there's a demon attached to the toy that is influencing your child's behavior, and your child has a soul tie with it.

If you want your child's behavior to change, you must address this issue. There are a few toys that I have already seen oppression come through. These toys are Pokémon, which stands for pocket monster, and the Lego toy Ninjago. Here is an article regarding Pokémon that might help you: https://www.spiritualwarfare.blog/pokemon; you can read about the concerns there. Ninjago, is a set of activities created around Lego characters that are Ninjas. The concerns with it come from the fact that a Ninja is defined as a "fighting spirit," the videos are constant blood-pumping action (which is addictive) and it is actually quite violent. (If you don't think that it's violent, I would consider if perhaps you have become numb or desensitized to violence yourself.) Ninjago, teaches children to be physically aggressive and watching anything with constant action can cause them to become addicted to adrenaline.

My children grew up watching Sesame Street, Barnie, Magic School Bus, Arthur, Veggie Tales and other *mostly* wholesome and educational shows. When you compare these shows with the violent action of Ninjago, perhaps you can see where I'm coming from. You might think, "Well, my kids are active, and they would be bored with those shows." If your kids are active, then get them outside to the park, on a trampoline or shooting hoops, not watching stuff that enforces over-stimulation and causes them to crave adrenaline. Children need to learn that calm activities are enjoyable too.

Some will say, "But it's only a game," or "It's only a toy." Yes. But what are you giving to that game or toy that is designed to prop up or elevate a worldview and spiritual perspective that is not godly? You are giving your money to purchase it, your time to play it or watch it, and you are giving it your attention, at the very least. If you are enjoying what you're doing, you're giving your affection to it also. Then, when you refuse to take it away from a child because it doesn't honor God, you are being disobedient to God and putting it in a high place—making it more important than Him.

Again, two steps: pray and purge. In this step, you will pray the prayer to break soul ties on behalf of your child, and you will repent for not governing your home as a godly leader by letting your child watch and listen to violence, play games that are violent, play games or watch videos so frequently they became addicted, or have toys that are connected to the occult or an *animistic* spiritual worldview[33] that is anti-Christian and anti-One-God in nature. (See endnote 32 to see what *animism* is.) **Do NOT** pray this with or around your children. Pray in a private space preferably with your spouse (if applicable). Your children do not have to be physically present to be affected by your prayer. There is no distance in the spirit realm.

Prayer

"Father, we/I thank You for (name of child). We/I thank You that You have blessed our lives with him/her and that You have given us authority as his/her parents over his/her life. We thank You, God, that You cause us to have victory over our enemies through the blood of Your Son, Jesus. And we celebrate that Jesus has ALREADY destroyed ALL the works and schemes of the devil, stripping him of his authority and putting him in his rightful place as the looser of every challenge for all time. We come to You, Father, in repentance with contrite hearts. Please forgive me/us for allowing games, toys, movies and videos into our home and into the hands of our children that are antichrist, anti-Christian, pay tribute to false gods, and may be demonic in nature—things that do not honor You, God, and do not teach or represent godly principles. Forgive us for allowing our children to consume violence and too much action that has caused them to be in a state of over-stimulation and "high" on adrenaline. We/I repent. And we/I ask for the blood of Your Son to wash us clean. Forgive us/me for not leading our/my family in Your ways. We/I renounce animism, all multiple-gods theology and beliefs, aggression, anger, hate, violence, murder, every demon associated with self-defence, addiction, the antichrist spirit, confusion, self-protection, the need to be entertained and the worship of entertainment. We/I repent on behalf of our/my children for consuming entertainment that does not honor You, Lord. Please forgive them. Thank You for Your forgiveness over us all. We receive it now. We/I renounce agreement with all these demonic entities and cut them off from us all now. We/I bind the power of all these demons, and we/I command them to leave us, leave our children, and leave our home right now, in Jesus' name. You will leave right now, and you will go to the feet of Jesus. We/I command every demon associated with animism, multi-God theology and beliefs, aggression, anger, hate, violence, murder, self-defence, self-protection, addiction, antichrist, confusion, and entertainment to come out and come off our/my children NOW, in Jesus' name. We/I break your power and command you to leave upon their natural breathing now and go to the feet of Jesus. Lord, we/I ask You to heal every wound in our hearts that caused us to seek out fulfillment with ungodly entertainment. Fill our children and us, Lord, with a fresh infilling of Your Spirit. Fill us completely, God. Thank You for what You're doing. Cause Your Spirit to surround our children to protect them. Show us now, Lord, what games, toys, videos, and movies need to be purged from our home. (Wait on God and write down what He shows you.)"

Break Soul Ties between your children and the toys, games etc the Lord showed you to remove from your home. Don't forget to put your faith behind these prayers:

"Lord, we/I thank You for *(say child's name)*. We/I thank You that You have given us as his/her parents authority over his/her life. So right now, we/I confess to You, Lord, on behalf of *(say child's name)* the emotional connection and reliance that *(say child's name)* has developed with *(say the name of the game/toy etc.)* and on his/her behalf, we/I repent. We/I ask You to forgive him/her for his/her reliance on it and his/her love for it. We ask You to pour out Your blood over him/her. Thank You, Lord, we receive Your forgiveness over him/her on his/her behalf. We/I now break and sever the emotional tie between *(say child's name)* and *(name of toy/game etc.)* in ALL its forms and we/I say that he/she will no longer see it as something he/she needs. We/I break all addiction to it, off him/her now, in Jesus' name. Every piece of his/her heart that she/he surrendered to *(name the game, toy etc.)* we call back to him/her now. Wash it in Your blood, Jesus, and make him/her whole in You. Thank You, God, for what You're doing in him/her right now as we speak. Thank You for restoring his/her heart to You. Give us/me the fortitude, resilience, and strength now, God, to purge our house as You have directed us/me. In Jesus' mighty name, amen."

Further Action

Now, it's time to purge your house, but before you just throw your children's toys away and cause trauma, pray and ask the Holy Spirit how to carry this out, then make a plan. I believe it's important that the children understand why you are doing this and why it needs to happen first, so they don't end up resentful and angry.

To assist with this process, please look for my series of companion story books for children coming out in 2025 called, *Alastair Companion Story Books*. These books will be all about a young boy named Alastair and how he goes from being afraid, hiding under his covers every night at bedtime and lashing out in anger, to being strong and courageous, as a child of God, facing his fears in the power of the Holy Spirit. These stories will be great tools in your toolbelt for teaching your children about God and His plan for our salvation, who the devil is and where he came from, how to hear and discern God's voice, and how we can overcome fear and anger with the spiritual weapons we've been given in Christ.

Prepare your child(ren) for what is about to happen. Pray and ask the Lord to give you His wisdom on how you approach this. Here are some suggestions you might want to consider:

- If you're using the Alastair story books, incorporate the books into a story time and teaching routine over the course of a few weeks. Plan to implement the purge of toys/games on a weekend when you feel you've successfully laid a foundation of understanding for the need to honor God well and not worship other things. Each time you embark on reading an Alastair story, pray ahead of time: "In Jesus' name, I bind and take authority over every demonic spirit that would want to interfere with this teaching, and I break its power. I say you will not act out or speak or disrupt our time together. I sanctify my time with *(say child's name)* right now and I declare the blood of Jesus over both of us now, in Jesus' name."
- Severely limit, as much as possible, the time that your children spend playing with the toys/games in question, until they are out of your house. You may find that after you pray the prayer above to break soul ties between your children and their toys, that they no longer have interest in them. Play that by ear. Perhaps getting rid of them will be easier than you expect.
- Begin the process on a Friday evening and continue Saturday. This way they have another day at home to process what happened before going back to school.

- Make sure your children understand that what God has asked your family to do may not be what other families need to do. Teach them to be humble and not self-righteous toward others. We should never look down on anyone for playing with the things God has told us to get rid of. We don't need to tell everyone what we are doing as not everyone will understand nor need to follow suit.
- Give them something new, wrapped as a gift, to replace what they are giving up.
- Make sure they don't view it as some sort of punishment for bad behavior.
- Let them see that you also are giving things up.
- Turn it into a fun family activity. Explain to them why the toys and games you're purging are bad or how they are linked to other gods.
- Give each child a Rubbermaid bin and the responsibility of gathering the things you've discussed.
- Incorporate a celebration of "new beginnings" with a cake or an assortment of candy to choose from.
- Get a new fun family board game that you can play together.
- Make sure they understand the blessing that will surely come to your household for being obedient to the Lord and loving Him first and foremost.
- Find alternative Christian shows they can watch (for example, Bibleman).
- Pray together as a family and re-commit your lives to Jesus, then ask Jesus to baptize you all in the Holy Spirit so you're all empowered to follow through on what God has called you to do.

- Make sure to tell your family members (and parents of children you invite to birthday parties) who will buy gifts for your children not to buy the toys/games that the Lord has convicted you about. You may need to draw some tough boundaries here but ask the Lord to give you the words and memorize them if you have to. Stand your ground with grace.
- Instruct your children not to play with these toys at their friends' homes. Teach them what to say to their friends should they be in a situation where they are pressured to conform. Give them permission to call you to be picked up early from a playdate should they need a way out of peer pressure. Encourage them to be honest with you about their experience at friends' homes by not scolding them if they failed to implement the plan.
- Pray with your child should they give into temptation and teach them how to repent and ask for forgiveness.
- When they are old enough, teach them how to stand in their authority in Jesus, renounce demons and command them to come out.

After you have purged your house of all the toys, games, videos, and merchandise the Lord has told you to purge, pray in and over *each* room of your house (including every child's bedroom), anointing all window frames and door frames with oil, going from room to room. It might be wise to do this while the children are sleeping or not at home. Pray something like:

> "Lord, thank You for what You have done. Thank You for leading us in purifying our home according to Your standards. We/I stand in the gap and repent for every sinful action that has taken place in this

room. Please forgive us, Lord. We choose to forgive ourselves for our own sinful actions in this room and we choose to forgive others for their sinful actions in this room. Lord, we call on Your great mercy to flow over us and in this place. Cause Your forgiveness to cleanse and cut off from this place all reaping of sinful actions. Thank You, God, for Your mercy.

And in the authority that You have given us, We/I stand against and resist every demonic spirit in this room. We/I command every demonic spirit in this room and atmosphere to leave now in Jesus' name. You no longer have any place here. Our home belongs to the Lord. Every demon in the air, every demon hiding in the corners, every demon attached to any object, you will leave now and go to the feet of Jesus where you belong. RIGHT NOW, GO! *(Continue to command spirits to leave until you sense it is done.)* Thank You, Father, for Your song of deliverance over us (Psalm 32:7).

We/I anoint this window and/or door with oil as a symbol of Your protection over our home and we/I dedicate this room to You. Come Holy Spirit and fill every square inch of this place with Your abiding presence and Your power. We/I say, "This place is set apart for You, God." In Jesus' name, amen."

In the next chapter, let's have a look at some possible root spirits and associated spirits that could be causing our children issues, and then we will pray our final prayer of release on behalf of our kids.

SPIRITS, ACCESS POINTS & SYMPTOMS

Finally, we are ready to begin to pray against the oppression of our children. In this chapter, I will first give you information on demonic root spirits plus which other spirits *could* be connected, as well as how they gain access, and possible symptoms. In our final prayer, we will first declare Who God is on our behalf and who we are in Him. Then we will follow a plan to repent on behalf of our ancestors, ask the Lord to forgive our children (if applicable), bind the root spirits, bind, renounce and cast out associated spirits from our children, cast out the root spirits, and then finally ask the Holy Spirit to fill our children, surround them and keep them safe. **Do not pray over your children or with your children present.** You will pray the prayers on your own in a private place while they are sleeping. Then you will gage the success of your prayers by how they behave the next day and days following.

Following are charts with all the information. You can decide which root spirits you need to come against in prayer. As you read through the symptoms, highlight the ones you see in your child; this will give you an indication of which ones you will need to pray against. (Also, as you read through, pay attention to the Holy Spirit and what He shows you. Perhaps there is something you need to deal with in your own life before praying against it for your children.)

Some of this information I have taken from a book by Pastor Douglas Carr. He has many books available about deliverance, but the one I am referencing is called, *Free Indeed from Root Spirits* (available on Amazon). I have only mentioned symptoms you may see in your young children, but there could be other symptoms in adults. As well, keep in mind, that just because your child has a condition mentioned, does not mean it is because of demonic oppression. Sometimes a physical condition is purely a physical issue. For example, ADD/ADHD is mentioned as a symptom in a few places, but it's not always caused by demonic oppression; sometimes it is a hormonal imbalance in the brain and nothing more. Other times, it *is* demonic oppression. When it is caused solely by demonic oppression, ADD/ADHD should cease after you've prayed against it and cast it out. However, I would suggest including prayer for healing over physical issues as well.

Root Spirit of Antichrist

| Associated Spirits: | doubt, unbelief, legalism, rebellion, disobedience, control, fear, manipulation, intimidation, disrespect, lawlessness, defiance, fighting, chaos, disorder, anger, |

Associated Spirits:	violence, murder, anxiety, dread, and more.
Scripture Reference:	1 John 4:1-3
Access Points:	Ancestral iniquity and/or sin related to legalism and the Pharisee spirit or involvement with false religion, cults, secret societies or the occult, atheism, blasphemy against God, false teaching, renouncing God, hatred toward God/Jesus/Holy Spirit, deep-rooted unforgiveness toward God, blaming God for the bad things in life and more.
Possible Symptoms:	Not wanting to go to church, not wanting to pray, saying things against God, not wanting to hear about God, disobedience, rebellion, defiance, hating God, fear, speaking threatening words, physical violence, and more.

Root Spirit of Fear

Associated Spirits:	Fear of the future (anxiety), fear of the dark, fear of bad dreams, fear of death, fear of rejection, fear of not belonging, fear of not fitting in, fear of abandonment, fear of not being liked, fear of not having friends, fear of other people and social settings, fear of not being seen, fear of not

Associated Spirits cont'd:	being heard, fear of..., dread, anger, despair, tragedy, woe, depression, stress, trauma, terror, and more.
Scripture Reference:	2 Timothy 1:7
Access Points:	Ancestral iniquity and/or sin involving abuse, threatening behavior or words, yelling, watching horror or occult movies about witches, warlocks or vampires, reading occult-themed books (Harry Potter, Twilight), involvement in the occult, playing occult games (Ouija Board, Magic Eight Ball, Bloody Mary and more), telling ghost stories and more.
Possible Symptoms:	Mental torment, intrusive thoughts, hearing voices, night terrors, sleep paralysis, agitation, anger, overly careful/cautious, depression, doubt, lack of trust, escapism, fantasy, excessively sensitive, frustration, headaches, migraines, hysteria, insecurity, inferiority complex, indecision, inadequacy, insomnia, loneliness, low self-esteem, paranoia, panic disorder, procrastination, reclusiveness, shyness, asthma, stuttering, teeth grinding, digestive problems, Crohn's disease, Colitis and more.

Root Spirit of Bondage

Associated Spirits:	Addiction, control, fear, unforgiveness, hate, anger, grief, and more
Scripture Reference:	Romans 8:15 & Galatians 5:1
Access Points:	Ancestral iniquity and/or sin connected to addictions, idolatry, gossip, temper, lying, anger, hate, or unforgiveness and more.
Possible Symptoms:	Cheating, lying, compulsive sin, fear of death, gossip, habitual talker, possibly ADD/ADHD, temper tantrums, addiction to games or anything else, mental health issues, anger, hate, refusing to forgive others, depression and more.

Deaf & Dumb Root Spirit

Associated Spirits:	Control, fear, paranoia, rebellion, disobedience, and more.
Scripture Reference:	Mark 9:17-27
Access Points:	Ancestral iniquity and/or sin connected to idolatry, abuse, rebellion, disobedience, and more.
Possible Symptoms:	Ear problems, chronic ear infections, hearing loss, not listening, not speaking (non-verbal), seizures, mental illness,

Possible Symptoms cont'd:	depression, eye problems, confusion, grinding teeth, mouth infections, stupor or a dazed state, stuttering, dizziness, tinnitus, learning disabilities and more.

Root Spirit of Hautiness/Pride

Associated Spirits:	Anger, hate, violence, rebellion, entitlement, stubbornness, unforgiveness, selfishness, defiance, hard-heartedness, cold-heartedness and more.
Scripture Reference:	Proverbs 16:18-19
Access Points:	Ancestral iniquity and/or sin connected to control, pride, anger, rage, hating others, being unteachable, not listening, rebellion against authority, stubborn, selfish, mistreating people, needing to have one's own way, injustice, holding onto offense, unforgiveness, abuse, narcissism and more.
Possible Symptoms:	Being angry, hating others, fits of rage, temper tantrums, being argumentative, habit of disagreeing, defiance, not wanting to learn, hitting, biting, yelling, throwing things, destroying things, harming animals, disobedience, complaining of things not being fair, always wanting to be first, always wanting the upper hand or

Possible Symptoms cont'd:	the bigger piece, selfishness, insisting on having own way, putting others down, being critical of others, not wanting to forgive others.

Root Spirit of Stupor/Slumber

Associated Spirits:	Unbelief, idolatry, disobedience, hard-heartedness, legalism, Pharisee spirit, antichrist, deaf and dumb spirit and more.
Scripture Reference:	Romans 11:8, Isaiah 29:10, Matthew 13:13-15
Access Points:	Ancestral iniquity and/or sin connected to not loving God first and foremost but putting other things or people above God, disobedience to God, not believing the Word of God, not trusting God, self-sufficiency, people pleasing, hypocrisy, not trusting the Holy Spirit, quenching the Holy Spirit, rejecting the HS, speaking against the HS, not believing in the baptism of the HS, blaspheming an authentic move of God, judging a true move of God as demonic, judging anointed ministers of the Gospel, speaking against anointed ministers of the Gospel.
Possible Symptoms:	Sleepiness, drowsiness, lack of focus, possibly ADD/ADHD, fatigue,

Possible Symptoms cont'd:	confusion, apathy, passivity, dizziness, laziness, anemia, sickness, hearing loss, loss of eyesight, loss of smell, loss of taste, chronic ear infections, easily distracted, can't understand the Bible, falls asleep when praying or reading the Bible, addiction to games, lack of spiritual discernment, not hearing the voice of God and more.

Root Spirit of Jealousy

Associated Spirits:	Rejection, anger, hate, unforgiveness, pride and more.
Scripture Reference:	Numbers 5:30
Access Points:	Ancestral iniquity and/or sin relating to being jealous of others, favoritism, comparison, poverty, lack, inferiority, and believing lies about oneself not being good enough or less than others and more.
Possible Symptoms:	Anger, fits of rage, temper tantrums, backbiting, argumentative, accusatory, belittling others, hate, competitiveness, criticism, hurting others, fighting, dissatisfaction, lying, fault finding, gossip, greed, hardness of heart and more.

Root Spirit of Heaviness

Associated Spirits:	Grief, despair, disappointment, hope deferred, dread, anxiety, hopelessness, helplessness, depression, rejection, and more.
Scripture Reference:	Isaiah 61:3
Access Points:	Ancestral iniquity and/or sin related to prolonged grief (not moving through it), fear, anxiety, worry, believing lies about oneself and/or their future and more.
Possible Symptoms:	Depression, anxiety, crying, loneliness, broken heart, critical, defeated mindset, fatigue, excessive sleeping, discouragement, despondency, negative expectations, laziness, pessimism, lack of interest, self-pity, shame, suicidal thoughts, mental torment, bad dreams, gluttony, poverty and more.

Root Spirit of Harlotry/Prostitution

Associated Spirits:	Lust, perversion, homosexuality, victimization, abuse, idolatry, adultery, and more.
Scripture Reference:	Hosea 4:12 NKJV

Access Points:	Ancestral iniquity of prostitution, incest, sexual abuse, paying off someone to be quiet about sexual abuse (bribery), buying someone gifts in exchange for sexual favors, adultery, idolatry (not putting God first), people pleasing, disobedience to God, worshipping idols, witchcraft, involvement in occult practices, and more.
Possible Symptoms:	Early interest in sex, homosexuality, bisexuality, victimization, sexual abuse & molestation, overactive sex drive, accidently seeing pornography, shame, masturbation, self-exposure, all sexual dysfunctions, and more.

Root Spirit of Lying

Associated Spirits:	Fear, deception, gossip, perversion, slander, control, manipulation, rejection, and more.
Scripture Reference:	1 Kings 22:22 & 2 Chronicles 18:22
Access Points:	Ancestral iniquity and sin connected to lying, fibbing, deception, exaggerating, taking advantage of someone, leading someone astray, embellishing stories, keeping secrets, manipulating others, twisting words, trying to control others, gossiping, slandering, bearing false

Access Points Cont'd:	witness, holding onto offence, lying because of fear, and more.
Possible Symptoms:	deceitfulness, deception, delusion, betrayal, exaggeration, excessive talking, accusing others, blaming others, slandering others, fantasy, telling stories with the intent to manipulate, gossip, fear of authority, perversity/twisting the truth, homosexuality, hypocrisy, perfectionism poor self-image, condemnation, performance mentality, pride, seeking approval, scheming, trickery, pretending, avoidance, and more.

Root Spirit of Death

Associated Spirits:	Fear, anxiety, tragedy, infirmity, weakness, sickness, pain, woe, violence, anger, murder, self-harm, self-hate, depression, heaviness, discouragement, despair, prolonged grief, and more.
Scripture Reference:	Exodus 12:23 & 12:29[34]
Access Points:	Ancestral iniquity connected to abortion, attempting to abort, murder, attempted murder, rejection of a baby in utero, death wish spoken over a baby in utero, severe physical abuse (choking), and more.

Possible Symptoms:	Violence, anger, abuse, physical fighting, sorrow, accidents, near-death accidents/illness, mental torment, nightmares, night terrors, asthma, fear of death, fascination with death, mistreatment of animals, self-harm, self-hate, suicidal thoughts, eating disorders, unusual deaths in the family, early death, chronic sickness, depression, despair, discouragement, prolonged grief and more.

Root Spirit of Infirmity

Associated Spirits:	Rejection, fear, hate, anger, early death, deaf & dumb, trauma, and more.
Scripture Reference:	Luke 13:11-13
Access Points:	Ancestral iniquity connected to unforgiveness, bitterness, anger, hatred, judgements, abuse, and more.
Possible Symptoms:	Weakness, sickness, chronic colds, chronic viruses, asthma, possibly ADD/ADHD, allergies, ongoing hereditary illnesses, arthritis, scoliosis, bronchitis, abnormal or excessive bleeding, cancer, hatred, seizures, digestive disorders, chronic skin issues, chronic ear infections, fainting, headaches, migraines, mental health issues, motion sickness, infections,

| Possible Symptoms Cont'd: | sinusitis, mental torment, Tourette Syndrome, deep emotional wounds/wounded spirit, rejection, and more. |

Root Spirit of Perversity

Associated Spirits:	Lust, deception, homosexuality, gender dysphoria, lying, iniquity, twisted thinking, logic, humanism, pride, fear, worry, anxiety, anger, hate, strife, and more.
Scripture Reference:	Isaiah 19:14
Access Points:	Ancestral iniquity and sin connected to lying, deception, lust, sexual molestation & abuse, pornography, sexual fantasy, incest, chronic masturbation, any type of sexual sin, believing false doctrine, teaching false doctrine, and more.
Possible Symptoms:	Filthy minded, gender dysphoria, homosexuality, lying, misunderstandings, confusion, worry, chronic masturbation, touching inappropriately, sexual molestation & abuse, hate, anger, jealousy, dirty language, inappropriate joke telling, foul mouth, and more.

Root Spirit of Divination

Associated Spirits:	Deception, pride, control, manipulation, fear, intimidation, rebellion, witchcraft, insecurity, anxiety, fear of the future, superstition, seduction, Pharisee spirit, error, and more.
Scripture Reference:	Acts 16:16
Access Points:	Ancestral iniquity and sin related to involvement in any occult activity, false religion, cult, or secret society, believing false doctrine, teaching false doctrine, astrology, seeking spiritual power, seeking to know the future, believing in and owning good luck charms, playing occult games (Ouija board, magic eight ball etc.), being entertained by occult themed movies/books, constantly seeking prophetic words from others to know the future, and more.
Possible Symptoms:	Fear, fear of the dark, nightmares, not wanting to go to sleep, dread, feeling like something bad is going to happen, seeing ghosts or shadows, and more.

Root Spirit of Error

Associated Spirits:	Deception, doubt, unbelief, fear, Pharisee spirit, antichrist, logic, humanism, pride, divination, confusion, and more.
Scripture Reference:	1 John 4:6
Access Points:	Ancestral iniquity and sin related to false doctrine, perversion or twisting of scripture, involvement in false religions, cults, secret societies, lying, being deceptive, compromising convictions, disobedience, and more.
Possible Symptoms:	Eating disorders, gender dysphoria, transgenderism, unable to make decisions, confusion, disobedience, disrespect, making bad decisions, and more.

Final Prayer

"Heavenly Father, thank You for Who You are. Thank You for Your goodness and Your mercy and grace over us (I am using "us" to refer to your family unit, so even if you are a single parent, use "us" to include your children). Thank You that You don't give us what our sins deserve, but You give us what we don't deserve. Thank You that You are faithful and that You never leave us nor forsake us. Thank You that You are trustworthy and longsuffering. We praise You and give You all the glory. We worship You and submit our lives and hearts to You completely. If there is any part of our hearts that we have not surrendered to You, please show us now. (Have a few moments of silence and listen for God to communicate to you anything He needs to. Should you discern the Spirit showing you something, surrender it to Him and repent for not surrendering it sooner.)

Lord, is there anything You have asked me/us to do that I/we haven't yet done? (Listen for God's response. If He shows you something, repent for not being obedient to what He asked you to do. If there is something you can do about it now, do it. For example, if God has shown you that you need to apologize to someone and you haven't done it yet, make a phone call and do it or at least commit to doing it at the next possible time. If there is a strained relationship that God has told you to reconcile, take a step toward that reconciliation now. Repent for procrastination. Repent for avoidance, and possibly fear and pride, plus whatever else the Spirit shows you. It's crucial that you are right with God before going further.)

Thank You, God, that we are Yours, that You sent Your Son, Jesus, to die for us, to pay the penalty of our sin, to set us free from the bondage of sin, and to destroy the works of the devil. Thank You that our lives are hidden in You, and we are safe covered in the blood of Your precious Son, Jesus.

We praise You God that You have completely defeated the devil by raising Jesus back to life and causing Him to reign with You. We declare Your complete victory over the devil and confirm that he is the loser for all time. We repent for ever agreeing with his perverted, twisted ways. Please forgive our ignorance. Thank You, Lord, again for Your mercy and grace. You, Lord, are The Light of our lives.

Repent on Behalf of Your Ancestors:

(Change pronouns as appropriate. If praying by yourself, use *I, me,* and *my*. However, if you are a married couple raising children, it's *preferable* to pray as a couple.) Lord, we confess to You now that our families have not honored You well. We have not lived lives of repentance nor given You first place in our hearts. As a family, we have broken Your heart, and we are sorry. We have worshipped other things, other gods, and ourselves. Please forgive us. Lord, our ancestors have committed heinous sins against one another. We have treated each other grievously—with great harm. On behalf of our ancestors, we repent and ask for Your forgiveness. Thank You, God. We choose right now to forgive our ancestors for their sin and for passing iniquity on to us. Thank You, God, that according to Galatians 3:13 Jesus has redeemed us from the curse of the law by becoming a curse for us as it is written, "Cursed is everyone who hangs on a tree." I thank You that right now any curse that has come through our ancestors' iniquity is broken and no longer provides any landing strip for the enemy. By the blood of Jesus and in His name, we cancel every opportunity the devil has had through iniquity to oppress our family. Thank You, God, for the complete cleansing of iniquity from our bloodline, back and forward through the generations, in Jesus' name.

Ask God to Forgive Your Kids (pray what applies):

Lord, we also stand in the gap for our kids, and we confess that our kids have walked in sin. They have been disobedient to You and us. They have been defiant and angry. They have operated in physical violence, hitting us and each other. They have lied to us, and they have been jealous of one another. They have held on to anger and unforgiveness in their hearts. They have hated..... They have...... (Add any other sin you know of and anything the Spirit puts on your heart.) Lord, please forgive them. We choose to forgive them for it all. And we thank You for Your mercy and forgiveness over them, in Jesus' name. We renounce their sin, and we claim the blood of Jesus over them now, cleansing them from all unrighteousness. (Give Him praise.) We declare that any landing strip in our kids for the devil, due to their sin, is removed now, in Jesus' name. The blood of Jesus covers them—purifies and cleanses them from all unrighteousness.

Bind Strongman Spirits:

Now, in the authority You have given us as Your children, we stand against and resist the devil just as You told us to do in James 4:7.

In the mighty name of Jesus, we bind and fully restrict every strongman demonic spirit that is oppressing us and our child(ren). We bind and renounce the root spirit of antichrist, fear, and bondage oppressing (say each child's name separately). In Jesus' name, we bind and renounce the deaf and dumb root spirit, and the root spirit of pride oppressing (say each child's name). In Jesus' name, we bind and renounce the root spirit of stupor, jealousy, heaviness, harlotry, lying, death, and infirmity oppressing (say each child's name). We also bind and renounce the root spirit of perversity, divination, and error oppressing (say each child's name), in Jesus' name. We forbid any of these root spirits to manifest in any way, or cause any of us harm, or interfere with what we are doing. You strongman spirits will not speak, and you will not cause any distress to us or our children. You have no voice. You have no power or authority here. The blood of Jesus is against you. We command every strongman demon and every lesser demon oppressing (say children's names) to disentangle from one another right now in Jesus' name. You will not reinforce one another anymore. We command you to be loosed from one another right now, in Jesus' name.

Bind, Restrict and Renounce:

(Pray through for each child separately) In the authority of Jesus, we bind, restrict, take authority over, and renounce all demonic spirits oppressing (say name of child).

Right now, we bind, restrict, take authority over and renounce every demon of doubt, unbelief, legalism, rebellion, disobedience, control, manipulation, intimidation, witchcraft, disrespect, lawlessness, defiance, fighting, chaos, disorder, anger, violence, murder, anxiety, and dread in or attached to *(say child's name)*.

In Jesus' name, we bind, restrict, take authority over, and renounce every demon of fear in or attached to *(say child's name)*. Specifically, we bind, restrict, take authority over, and renounce every demon of the fear of the dark, fear of bad dreams, fear of death, fear of rejection, fear of not belonging, fear of not fitting in, fear of abandonment, fear of not being liked, fear of not having friends, fear of other people and social settings, fear of not being seen, fear of not being heard, fear of the future, fear of poverty, fear of lack, fear of .... *(list all his/her fears)* in or attached to *(say child's name)*.

In Jesus' name, we bind, restrict, take authority over, and renounce every demon of tragedy, woe, despair, depression, stress, trauma, terror, affliction, addiction, unforgiveness, hate, paranoia, entitlement, selfishness, stubbornness, hard-heartedness, cold-heartedness, idolatry, rejection and pride attached to or in *(say child's name)*.

In Jesus' name, we bind, restrict, take authority over, and renounce every demon of grief, disappointment, hope deferred, hopelessness, helplessness, lust, seduction, homosexuality, adultery, gender dysphoria, victimization, abuse, false guilt, deception, confusion, gossip, gluttony, stealing, kleptomania, and slander attached to or in *(say child's name)*.

In Jesus' name, we bind, restrict, take authority over, and renounce every demon of weakness, sickness, pain, self-harm, self-hate, discouragement, logic, humanism, strife, worry, superstition, poverty and lack attached to or in *(say child's name)*.

Cast Out Minions (lesser spirits):

In the authority of Jesus and in His name, we command all these demonic spirits to leave *(say child's name)* right now as she/he sleeps. We say your time is up. You will leave right now on her/his natural breathing, and you will not cause her/him any harm or distress. The blood of Jesus covers her/him, and she/he belongs to the Lord.

Demon of doubt, unbelief, legalism, rebellion, disobedience, control, manipulation, intimidation, witchcraft, disrespect, lawlessness, defiance, fighting, chaos, disorder, anger, violence, murder, anxiety, and dread we/I call you up and out of *(say child's name)*. GO NOW! In Jesus' name. Leave on her/his natural breathing right now. *(In faith, believe and see this happening in your mind's eye.)* You will go to the feet of Jesus and never come back.

Demon of the fear of the dark, fear of bad dreams, fear of death, fear of rejection, fear of not belonging, fear of not fitting in, fear of abandonment, fear of not being liked, fear of not having friends, fear of other people and social settings, fear of not being seen, fear of not being heard, fear of the future, fear of poverty, fear of lack, fear of .... (list all other fears) we/I call you up and out of *(say child's name).* GO NOW! In Jesus' name. Leave on her/his natural breathing right now. *(In faith, believe and see this happening in your mind's eye.)* You will go to the feet of Jesus and never come back.

Demon of tragedy, woe, despair, depression, stress, trauma, terror, affliction, addiction, unforgiveness, hate, paranoia, entitlement, selfishness, stubbornness, hard-heartedness, cold-heartedness, idolatry, rejection and pride we/I call you up and out of *(say child's name).* GO NOW! In Jesus' name. Leave on her/his natural breathing right now. *(In faith, believe and see this happening in your mind's eye.)* You will go to the feet of Jesus and never come back.

Demon of grief, disappointment, hope deferred, hopelessness, helplessness, lust, seduction, homosexuality, adultery, gender dysphoria, victimization, abuse, false guilt, deception, confusion, gossip, gluttony, stealing, kleptomania, and slander we/I call you up and out of *(say child's name).* GO NOW! In Jesus' name. Leave on her/his natural breathing right now. *(In faith, believe and see this happening in your mind's eye.)* You will go to the feet of Jesus and never come back.

Demon of weakness, sickness, pain, self-harm, self-hate, discouragement, logic, humanism, strife, worry, superstition, poverty and lack we/I call you up and out of *(say child's name).* GO NOW! In Jesus' name. Leave on her/his natural breathing right now. *(In faith, believe and see this happening in your mind's eye.)* You will go to the feet of Jesus and never come back

Cast Out Root Spirits:

Finally, in the authority of Jesus and in His name, we command every root spirit to leave *(say child's name)* right now as she/he sleeps. We say your time is up. You will leave right now on her/his natural breathing, and you will not cause her/him any harm or distress. The blood of Jesus covers her/him, and she/he belongs to the Lord.

Demon of antichrist, fear, bondage, deaf and dumb, haughtiness, pride, stupor, jealousy, heaviness, harlotry, lying, death, infirmity, perversity, divination, and error we/I call you up and out of *(say child's name)*. GO NOW! In Jesus' name. Leave on her/his natural breathing right now. *(In faith, believe and see this happening in your mind's eye.)* You will go to the feet of Jesus and never come back.

Ask God to Fill Your Child:

Father, we now ask You to send Your Holy Spirit to fill and baptize (say child's name) afresh with Your presence and power. Heal every wound in her/his soul and occupy every place in her/his mind, will, and emotions, and every cell in her/his body. Completely saturate her/him in You, Lord.

Invite God to Heal:

We ask You, God, to heal any damage and every effect in (say child's name) body that the demons have had. Bring her/his spine and vertebrae into order and alignment. Heal her/his digestive tract, from the top to the bottom. Heal his/his nervous system. Heal every effect of stress and bring her/him back to homeostasis, out of fight or flight mode. Heal the neurotransmitters and pathways in (say child's name) brain. Bring her/his brain into complete order and hormonal balance, God, with the correct amount of dopamine, serotonin and every other hormone necessary for mental health. We/I speak and command complete divine healing over each cell of her/his body, in Jesus' name. We call divine order and balance to come to every system in her/his body, in Jesus' name. We command all inflammation to go, in Jesus' name. We command all pain to go, in Jesus' name. Thank You, Father. Thank You that Your Son Jesus has already paid the price for her/his complete healing and deliverance. Thank You, Father, that You finish what You start, and You never leave anything half-done. We/I look forward to seeing how You have transformed and healed (say child's name). Help us to parent her/him well. Open our eyes to see how special You have made (say child's name) and help us to know her giftings and the special abilities You've given her/him. Help us to steward them well and to encourage them in her/him. Give us wisdom and creative ideas on effect discipline that will guide and teach her/him well without crushing her/his heart or discouraging her/him. Help us to be humble and develop a heart-to-heart connection with all our children.

We give You all the praise, and all the glory for what You have already done, what You are doing now, and what You are about to do. We fix our eyes on You, Jesus, the author and finisher of our faith. In Your name we pray, amen."

FOLLOW THROUGH

"Once all of this is done, how do we move forward?" is a very important question to ask yourself and I'd like to give you some tips. I keep seeing in my mind a ship or a large sailboat that once was capsized being right side up again. This is awesome. Your family is that ship and it's now upright, but now you need to move that ship forward on the correct course with Jesus. You need to begin to take the responsibility for your child(ren)'s spiritual development. It is not the church's responsibility; it is yours. The world is simply too dark now for you not to train your children up in the ways of God and teach them how to have a heart connection with Jesus and the Holy Spirit. It is best to begin this when they are young.

Teach your children how to pray—how to have a *two-way* conversation with the Lord. Don't teach them wrote prayers. Teach them to share their heart with God. If they have not yet surrendered their heart to Jesus, teach them about God and then lead them to salvation in Jesus. Then teach them that the Spirit of Jesus wants to talk to them through their thoughts and spirit.

In addition, teach them the following things:

- To share their feelings with God each day, especially their anger. It is very important that we don't store up anger in our heart, so every day, teach them to tell God about it and then let God speak to them in return. As a visual exercise to help them see that they are giving their feelings to God, make up slips of paper with a feeling written on each. Have them take the slip of paper which corresponds to the feeling they need to give to God, and have them tell God about it. "Jesus, today I felt angry because ...... He/She hurt my feelings. They cut in line in front of me and I never got my turn..... etc. etc. It wasn't fair and it made me angry." When they are done telling God about it, they can rip up the paper and put it in the trash and say, "I give my anger to you Jesus and I ask you to take it away. Change my heart to be like yours." Then ask the child to hear what Jesus is saying back to him/her, or notice how Jesus is making them feel, or if they can visualize Jesus in their mind, ask them what they see Jesus doing.
- Who they are in Christ; how they have been changed inside by the Spirit of God.
- How to confess their sin to God.
- How to repent; what repentance is and why it's important.
- To repent everyday as needed or as soon as they are convicted. Teach them what conviction is and that it comes from the Holy Spirit.

- To forgive themselves.
- That hating people is wrong and that we need to forgive.
- How to forgive others in prayer and why that's important.
- How to love people who are difficult to love and why that's important.
- How to deal with fear. (Tell God about it, renounce it and tell it to go away.)
- The power of their words and positive declarations about who they are in Christ. Give them a few to memorize and say over themselves (from scripture) so they can fight against any negative thoughts being fed to them by the enemy.
- To read their Bible and hear God speak to them through it.
- To put others first and to think of themselves less.
- To understand the spirit realm and how to fight with faith and the Word.
- About the armor or God and how to wear it.
- Anything else the Holy Spirit leads you to teach them about spiritual matters.

Again, I hope to have a series of children's books out in 2025 which you will be able to use for their training. But you are your child's best teacher and best spiritual mentor. They not only receive your teaching, but they also pay close attention to what you do. So, make sure you are modeling to them what you are teaching. Your behavior speaks louder than your words.

With the Holy Spirit in you and with you, I know you're going to do great. You're anointed to be a mother/father and you're anointed to parent the children you have.³⁵ If you weren't, the Lord would not have given them to you.

CONCLUSION

Well, congratulations! You've come a long way. And you've been courageous as you've stepped out in boldness and in the authority Jesus has given you. Today marks the beginning of a brand-new parenting journey for you. It won't be the same as before. Praise God! I encourage you to continue to stand in your authority moving forward and if you need to go back and redo parts of the book that perhaps you may not have engaged fully with, do that. If you don't see the results you need, ask the Holy Spirit what part you need to revisit. Do not under any circumstances believe the lie that this process is a waste of time or doesn't work; that my friend is the father of lies filling your mind with garbage. This process absolutely works when done in faith and in connection to the Spirit of God because it's His power on your words that actually cause the transformation. And we know how powerful God is!

A very important key in this whole process is to be able to discern the leading of the Lord, whether it be hearing His voice in your thoughts or having an impression in your spirit (or *gut* as some might say). Jesus told us that His sheep would know and hear His voice (John 10:16) so if you're having trouble hearing His voice or discerning His leading, perhaps it's because you believe the lie that you *can't* hear His voice, or you *don't* hear His voice. Not true, my friend! We need to get this straight. The Word of God (the Bible) says you CAN hear His voice, so *believe* it. Believe God over everything else. He is speaking to you *somehow* and it's likely that you just don't realize that it's Him speaking.

Perhaps you think all the thoughts in your mind are you. But they're not! Some of them are God leading you. Ask the Lord to help you discern when it's Him and spend more time reading the Gospels (Matthew, Mark, Luke, and John) where Jesus speaks to us directly, to get to know the sound of His voice.

Lastly, this book has been written mostly for families with young children. If your child(ren) are over eighteen years old, and following the Lord, you can very much use the same prayers to take authority over any spirits that may be harassing them, however, I think I would add *identificational repentance* to my prayers which means you are standing in intercession and repenting on behalf of your child(ren) for the sins they may have committed. This type of repentance does not mean that they don't need to repent for themselves, but it does open a window of opportunity for the Lord to move in their life. For example, you can pray, "Lord I stand in the gap for ….. and I repent for cursing and lying" or whatever it is you sense they need to repent for but leave it up to the Holy Spirit to convict your older child(ren) of their sin. It does not help your older child for you to be reminding them of all they've done wrong; it only causes condemnation, which is not love. It is the kindness of God that will lead them to repentance.

If your adult child has not yet surrendered their life to Jesus, do identificational repentance, pray for their salvation, ask the Holy Spirit to surround them and brood over them, bind the demons, declare that they are mute, but do *not* tell demons to leave them. It is important for your child to be saved and filled with the Holy Spirit before you cast demons out or the demons will just come back even stronger because of the sin in their lives. As an example, you could pray the following: "Lord, I stand in the gap for ..... and I repent for ...... Lord, in Your mercy, please forgive her/him. In Your love and gentleness convict him/her. Holy Spirit, I ask that You would surround (child's name) and brood over him/her like a mother hen broods over her chicks to cause the re-birth and salvation of her heart through Jesus. As (child's name) mother/father and the authority I have in Jesus, I bind and restrict all demons from operating in (child's name) life. I bind and take authority over the demon of (name the demon) and I declare it mute, in Jesus' name. Demon of (name) you will not speak, and you will not cause (child's name) harm or strife; I break your power now, in Jesus' name. I cancel every assignment against (child's name) in the authority of Jesus and I declare (child's name) is now spiritual fruit, ripe for the picking. She/He is open to hear the conviction of the Lord and will respond to Him, in Jesus' mighty name. No demon in hell will stop it. Thank you, Jesus. Amen" Pray this as often as the Holy Spirit leads you.

I hope this bit of direction for your older children is helpful and brings them all the way into the Kingdom where they belong.

Finally, I am excited for how your life and the lives of your whole family will be forever changed because of your willingness and obedience to follow the Lord closer and take your stance against the schemes of the enemy. God has made you to be a warrior. He has made you to be strong and courageous in Him. And He has given you all the tools and weapons you need to be victorious.

I declare over you today that you are *more* than a conqueror in Christ Jesus. No weapon formed against you will prosper and absolutely nothing can separate you or prevent you from experiencing the love, care, and protection of our great and mighty God—Jehovah Rapha, the Lord our Healer; Jehovah Shalom, the Lord Who is our Peace; El Roi, the Lord Who sees you and comes to your aid without fail.

In conclusion, I bless you and declare that everything that has been accomplished is sealed in the blood of Jesus and will forever stand without loss or slipping backward in any way. I say the blood of Jesus covers you, your family, and your home and His great mercy will keep you and protect you according to His will, love, and trustworthy heart.

With all the love which is in Christ, thank you for allowing me to speak into your life and honoring the gift Christ has given me. May all the blessings of the Lord following you and chasing you down, overtake you continually.

Now to Him who is able
to keep you from stumbling,
And to present you faultless
Before the presence of
His glory with exceeding joy,
To God our Savior,
Who alone is wise,
Be glory and majesty,
Dominion and power,
Both now and forever.
Amen.
(Jude 1:24-25 NKJV)

NOTE FROM THE AUTHOR

I'm sure the journey through this book has been a challenging one—one of reflection and exposure that may have felt like an unwanted magnifying glass over the wounded places of your soul. I know and it's okay to feel a little beaten up through it, but I promise, if you persevere, victory will come. Please remember, there is no condemnation for those who are in Christ Jesus.

What qualifies me to write such a book? It's a good question. I have no seminary degree and no letters after my name, but neither did the apostles in the New Testament. They had training in the law but no training in grace—no training in the new covenant Jesus came with, but yet they moved in supernatural power spreading the gospel throughout the Mediterranean world. No, the world does not qualify me nor do men. Jesus does. The call of God on my life, does. And He equips me to fulfill His call.

From the moment I was saved at twenty-two years of age, God has shown up in power, awakening my spiritual senses to Him and the spiritual world around me. I have walked through many things and have had to confront many demons in my own life. I have lived the journey you've walked through in this book. I have lived it thus far for thirty-six years... and counting.

I was raised in one of the cults listed in this book—one that didn't even believe in the devil at all. As a result, I was pushed around by him without even knowing it, without even feeling it. The devil masqueraded as an angel of light very convincingly, but when I learned about the true identity of Jesus and why He died on the cross, I surrendered to Him immediately. I knew that He was what was missing in my life. However, the truth that the devil does exist was a very difficult pill to swallow. It was a truth that was very unsettling to me, and I desperately needed to know who I was in Christ to be at peace. God graciously led me to the book, *Victory Over the Darkness* by Neil T. Anderson which armed me with the truth I needed. Since then, I have cemented myself in my true identity as a daughter of God and stood boldly in the authority He has given me through His Son, Jesus. I will not leave any gift God has given me unopened. I will not leave any benefit of the cross—anything my Jesus suffered and died for—laying aside in the dust unvalidated and inactivated. I will, with God's help, live and move and have my being in the fullness of truth. I pray that you will join me.

Beloved, growing, maturing, and being transformed into the image of Christ is not an easy journey. It's a lot of being stretched out of your comfort zone, letting go of what you thought you knew, being courageous enough to know what you didn't want to know, being willing to be misunderstood by the world, and a lot of bowing low to the ground in humility. It's definitely not a place for pride, but a place for complete surrender. I pray that you are willing to embrace it. And if you are, let me just say, "Welcome to the true church of Jesus Christ. Welcome to the remnant. You are now an oil carrier who will have enough oil to last through the night and into the brightness of the new day to come."

ABOUT THE AUTHOR

Barbara Jane grew up in a family of five attending a Christian Science church until the age of twenty-two when the Lord, Jesus, called her into His fold. She has now never been so grateful for the transformation the Lord began in her life in that moment of revelation and salvation. It was a moment when everything clicked into place and everything she knew about God became crystal clear and made sense; the revelation of Jesus Christ was the missing piece. The years that followed would prove to be life altering and internally transforming in many ways.

Through her thirty-six years of faith in Christ thus far, she has had to face and renounce many things that tainted her family line like the antichrist spirit, the spirit of error and deception, lies, abuse in many forms, deep anger, hate, unforgiveness, bitter judgements, vows to self, disappointment, rejection, self-loathing, and despair. As she has walked out of agreement with darkness, breakthrough has been had in different areas of life including her ability to conceive and bear natural children. Because of the goodness and healing of the Lord, Barbara Jane had four amazing children—one beautiful girl and three handsome boys, who are now all thriving adults. In addition, she and her husband now have a wonderful daughter-in-law who makes a lovely addition to their original four.

It is with great honor that Barbara Jane pours out to her readers the knowledge, wisdom, and understanding that the Lord has poured into her. And it is her prayer that the time, love, and effort she has put into her books brings about great blessing and transformation in the lives of others. There is nothing more gratifying to Barbara than being used of the Lord to assist the Bride of Christ in getting ready for her big day of finally becoming perfectly united with her bridegroom, Jesus Christ.

Barbara has written four other books you might be interested in. They are as follows:

Barren No More: Prayer Strategy for Every Believer Experiencing Fertility Challenges

Key to Fertility: Rewriting Your Stories for Success in Conceiving and Birthing Babies

Sweet Sorrow: Surviving the Emotional Waves of Releasing Your Son to His Bride

Position Yourself for Healing: Finding the Sweet Spot Where Healing Becomes Reality

All can be purchased on Amazon.

APPENDIX A

There is an excellent teaching by Linda Heidler from a conference that was held in February of 2015 at Apostle Chuck Pierce's church, Glory of Zion, called, "Reversing the Effects of Freemasonry." Go to YouTube to view the full teaching so that you are informed. The following is the link:

https://www.youtube.com/watch?v=8Z-D8bY6rS8

(go ahead and advance the video past the worship segment if you so desire). This link may only be available for a certain amount of time. Hopefully you can catch it. Here is the prayer she prays at the end of the video to lead you into freedom from Freemasonry and ALL its affects:

"Lord, I come to you in the authority of Jesus, and I renounce all involvement with witchcraft and Freemasonry in my family right now and I stand before you God as one who wants my soul, mind, will, emotions, strength, and body, totally submitted and committed to you. I stand before you God, as your daughter/son—as one who has been bought by your blood, who has been set apart for you and by you. Lord, where my true identity in you was exchanged for a false identity, or where I allowed a false identity to be imposed on me and where my true authority in you was stolen and replaced by false authority, I repent of it and renounce it now and I say, "give it back!" Right now, I take back my God-given identity that He created for me, and I take back the God-given authority that He has invested in me as His child and co-heir. Lord, where I have relinquished my God-given value or where it was stripped away from me, where I have been subjected to a value system that required me to perform and work hard in order to prove my worth or to feel like I was worth anything at all, I renounce it and I break away from that system right now; that is not the truth of God. I do not agree with it anymore. I reject the belief that I have to work, strive or prove my worth in order to be loved and I declare that my worth comes from God, and I am worthy of love simply because He made me. I take back my God-given, unique, intrinsic value and worth right now in Jesus' name. I throw out that slipshod slipper and I put on what God has given me. I declare that my feet are shod with the shoes of the gospel of peace and that I am prepared to share that peace wherever I go. I declare that I am sure footed, and that God has given me hinds' feet—feet that are able to walk in high places without intimidation or fear—feet that are swift, agile, and nimble in order to navigate any terrain and escape any trap. I declare that I am able to leap and run into my destiny with God and when I see the vision, I am going to run for it and not be worried about being tripped up by any slipshod slipper. Right now, I pull off that hoodwink and I take back my mind, my eyes, my ears, and my mouth. I now open my eyes, ears, and mouth and I declare that I am free to think, see, hear, and speak the way God wants me to. My spiritual senses are completely open to discern what God wants me to discern. I grab hold of my access to the mind of Christ and the wisdom of God, and I am going to expect and allow God to transform and conform my mind to the mind of Christ without hindrance. I am ripping off this noose from around my neck that has caused me to be in bondage and under the control of a freemason spirit; I am not going to be led around by any false worship system or spirit anymore. I declare that my heart and soul are now free to follow the leading of the Holy Spirit and that ugly spirit that opposes and hates the Holy Spirit is not going to have any influence or control over me anymore. I take away that dagger from my chest and I decide right now that I will no longer guard my emotions or be fearful of expressing myself. I choose to release my emotions, and I declare that I am going to know the joy of the Lord and the joy of my salvation. I am going to know the compassion of Jesus; I'm going to know the love of God like I've never known it before. Where I have been blocked from knowing the love that God has for me, I'm not going to be blocked anymore. I am going to freely receive the love of God. I repent and renounce the words spoken by my family member before me, when they said they were "seeking the light of Freemasonry." Right now, I pull that dark cover off of my spirit and I take back my spirit that was made to commune with my Heavenly Father, to commune with the Holy Spirit—that was made to receive revelation from Him. I take back my spirit and declare that it is free to commune with God and receive from Him and I ask you, Lord, for new levels of communion and revelation. Right now, I renounce and break all of the oaths and vows and curses spoken against my body, and I take back the health that you pre-ordained and purchased for me, God. I take back the strength in my body that you want me to have. Your Word says that your Spirit living inside of me quickens my mortal body and causes me to be in health. Lord, I know that my body is important to you as it is your temple, so I refuse to have my body infested with sickness, disease, weakness, or infirmity. I take back what you have given to me and what is rightfully mine, in Jesus' name.

I declare that I have repented of all participation in the ceremonies of Freemasonry. I have renounced the spiritual transactions that took place in those ceremonies. I have reclaimed my God given identity, worth, and destiny. I have reclaimed my soul, mind, emotions, will, and senses. I have reclaimed my physical body. I have reclaimed my spirit. I have broken all covenant agreements with the false religious system of Freemasonry.

I now submit myself, body, soul, and spirit to the living God, the God of Israel, Maker of heaven and earth. I fully enter into covenant with Him. I now position myself in active resistance to the devil. According to the Word of God: Submit to God, resist the devil, and he must flee (James 4:7)! I claim my right to every blessing of God in place of the curses that have been affecting my life. The Word of God says that the blessing of God will overtake me. Healing, prosperity, favor, protection, power, wisdom, and all the blessings of God are now free to come on me and my children. I am unhindered by any connection to false worship. I now freely enter a new level of worship of the true and living God and of Jesus, His only Son with all my heart, soul, mind, and strength. I WILL go to new realms of worship in the Spirit and will join with angels in worshipping You, Lord. I will fulfill the destiny for which I was created. I will storm the gates of hell and prevail. Hallelujah! Amen."[36]

I would also add:

"I choose to forgive every ancestor who participated in Freemasonry or any other secret society; I forgive them for every curse and oath they spoke against me, my body, and my children and their bodies. I forgive them for activating curses against us and I forgive every person who deceived them, leading them into the secret society, and leading them while in it. I choose to forgive every person who led their initiation ceremony, and I pray also for their families as well—that they would be set free from Freemasonry too, in Jesus' name. Amen"

REFERENCES

Anderson, Neil T. *Victory Over the Darkness*. Bloomington, Minnesota: Bethany House, 2014.

Carr, Dr. Douglas E. *Free Indeed from Root Spirits*. Sturgis, Michigan: Doug Carr Freedom Ministry, 2014.

Chapman, Gary. *The Five Love Languages: The Secret to Love that Lasts*. Chicago, Illinois: Northfield Publishing, 2024.

De Simon, Barbara. *Position Yourself for Healing: Finding the Sweet Spot Where Healing Becomes Reality*. Windsor, Ontario: Barbara De Simon, 2022, 2024.

Dobson, Dr. James. *Temper Your Child's Tantrums*. Carol Stream, Illinois: Tyndale Momentum, 1986.

Idleman, Kyle. *gods at War: The Battle for Your Heart That Will Define Your Life*. Louisville, Kentucky: City on a Hill Productions, 2012. DVD.

Kendrick S., Kendrick A., Alcorn R. *The Resolution for Men*. Nashville, Tennessee: Kendrick Bros. LLC, 2011.

Martin, Walter. *The Kingdom of the Cults*. Minneapolis, Minnesota: Bethany House Publishers, 1965, 1977, 1985, 1997.

Prince, Derek. *They Shall Expell Demons: What You Need to Know about Demons—Your Invisible Enemies*. Bloomington, Indiana: Chosen Books, 1998, 2020.

Shirer, Priscilla. *The Armor of God*. Brentwood, Tennessee: Lifeway Christian Resources, 2022.

Shirer, Priscilla. *The Resolution for Women*. Nashville, Tennessee: Kendrick Bros. LLC, 2011.

https://www.blueletterbible.org/

https://uxdesign.cc/fenced-in-playgrounds-d5f9371f8414

https://www.truthandfreedomchurch.com/post/deliverance-ministry-can-a-christian-have-a-demon-and-need-deliverance

https://www.ekhartyoga.com/

https://biblehub.com

https://www.merriam-webster.com

https://anthropologyreview.org/

ENDNOTES

[1] Numbers 6:24-26, "The LORD bless you and keep you; The LORD make his face shine upon you, And be gracious to you; The LORD lift up His countenance upon you, And give you peace" (NKJV).

[2] Matt. 4:24, Matt. 8:16, Matt. 8:28-32, Matt. 9:32-33, Matt. 12:22, Matt. 15:22-28, and Matt. 17:18.

[3] "Behold, I give you the authority to trample on serpents and scorpions, and over all the power of the enemy, and nothing shall by any means hurt you" (Luke 10:19 NKJV).

[4] https://uxdesign.cc/fenced-in-playgrounds-d5f9371f8414

[5] Dr. James Dobson, *Temper Your Child's Tantrums* (Carol Stream: Tyndale Momentum, 1986) 6. Print.

[6] Genesis 2:16-17, "And the LORD God commanded the man, "You are free to eat from any tree in the garden; but you must not eat from the tree of the knowledge of good and evil, for when you eat from it you will certainly die" (NIV).

[7] 1 John 1:9, "If we confess our sins, He is faithful and just to forgive us our sins and to cleanse us from all unrighteousness" (NKJV).

[8] Proverbs 17:22, "A happy heart is good medicine and a joyful mind causes healing, But a broken spirit dries up the bones" (AMP).

[9] https://www.blueletterbible.org/lexicon/g1139/kjv/tr/0-1/

[10] Google dictionary

[11] Derek Prince, *They Shall Expel Demons: What You Need to Know about Demons—Your Invisible Enemies* (Bloomington: Chosen Books, 1998, 2020) 25. Print.

[12] www.blueletterbible.org/Comm/smith_chuck/c2000_Eph/Eph_005.cfm?a=1102018

[13] https://en.wikipedia.org/wiki/Daniel_David_Palmer#Spiritualism

[14] James 5:12, "Above all, my brothers and sisters, do not swear [an oath]—not by heaven or by earth or by anything else. All you need to say is a simple "Yes" or "No." *Otherwise you will be condemned*" (NIV, brackets and italics added).

[15] Deuteronomy 18:9-13, "When you enter the land the LORD your God is giving you, do not learn to imitate the detestable ways of the nations there. Let no one be found among you who sacrifices their son or daughter in the fire, who practices divination or sorcery, interprets omens, engages in witchcraft, or casts spells, or who is a medium or spiritist or who consults the dead. Anyone who does these things is detestable to the LORD; because of these same detestable practices the LORD your God will drive out those nations before you. You must be blameless before the LORD your God" (NIV).

[16] https://www.merriam-webster.com/dictionary/cult

[17] https://www.merriam-webster.com/dictionary/spurious

[18] Walter Martin, The Kingdom of the Cults (Minneapolis: Bethany House Publishers, 1965, 1977, 1985, 1997) 17. Print.

[19] Barbara De Simon, Position Yourself for Healing: Finding the Sweet Spot Where Healing Becomes Reality (Windsor: Barbara De Simon, 2024) 62. Print.

[20] Priscilla Shirer, The Armor of God: Session 3 (www.lifeway.com: Lifeway Christian Resources) 2022. Video.

[21] 1 Corinthians 12:7-11, "Now to each one the manifestation of the Spirit is given for the common good. To one there is given through the Spirit a message of wisdom, to another a message of knowledge by means of the same Spirit, to another faith by the same Spirit, to another gifts of healing by that one Spirit, to another miraculous powers, to another prophecy, to another distinguishing between spirits, to another speaking in different kinds of tongues, and to still another the interpretation of tongues. All these are the work of one and the same Spirit, and he distributes them to each one, just as he determines" (NIV).

[22] 1 Corinthians 14:3, "But he who prophesies speaks edification and exhortation and comfort to men" (NKJV).

[23] Gary Chapman, The Five Love Languages: The Secret to Love that Lasts (Chicago: Northfield Publishing, 2024). Print.

[24] https://www.ekhartyoga.com/articles/practice/6-sacred-yoga-poses

[25] Stephen Kendrick, Alex Kendrick, and Randy Alcorn, The Resolution for Men (Nashville: Kendrick Bros. LLC, 2011) Introduction. eBook.

[26] https://biblehub.com/commentaries/ephesians/6-4.htm
[27] Kendrick, Kendrick, Alcorn, *The Resolution for Men*, Introduction. eBook.
[28] Kendrick, Kendrick, Alcorn, *The Resolution for Men*, Introduction, eBook.
[29] Kendrick, Kendrick, Alcorn, *The Resolution for Men*, Introduction, eBook.
[30] Ephesians 5:25, "Husbands, love your wives, just as Christ loved the church and gave himself up for her..." (NIV).
[31] Priscilla Shirer, *The Resolution for Women* (Nashville: Kendrick Bros. LLC) 278. eBook.
[32] Romans 8:34, "...It is Christ who died, and furthermore is also risen, who is even at the right hand of God, who also makes intercession for us"(NKJV).
[33] If you're wondering what animism is, it is the belief that all things—people, animals, trees, rocks etc. have spirits and spiritual power, thereby being able to influence what happens in your life and in the world, which is why some people believe in the god of the volcano or the god of the wind. Here's a quote I found: "In many animistic traditions, spirits are believed to have their own personalities and desires. They may be benevolent or malevolent, helpful or harmful. Spirits are also thought to be capable of influencing events in the world around us, <u>making offerings and rituals designed to appease them</u> an important part of many animistic practices."https://anthropologyreview.org/anthropology-glossary-of-terms/animism-the-belief-that-all-things-have-a-spirit/ This is demonic and the belief that there are many gods.
[34] The Bible does not refer to the spirit that killed all of Egypt's firstborn sons and livestock at the first Passover as a "spirit of death," however it does refer to it as "the destroyer," and I believe it is reasonable to see this spirit as a "spirit of death." We know that God has the enemy on a leash (see Job 1) and God is in control, not the devil. This is why the text says that God sent the death spirit out among the Egyptians.
[35] Just want to give a shout out to my good friend, Rosie, for always encouraging us moms in this way.
[36] Linda Heidler, *Reversing the Effects of Freemasonry*, YouTube. https://www.youtube.com/watch?v=8Z-D8bY6rS8.

Manufactured by Amazon.ca
Bolton, ON

43615783R00151